Foundation
Teacher's Book

GCSE English/English Literature

Roger Lane

OXFORD
UNIVERSITY PRESS

Great Clarendon Street, Oxford OX2 6DP

Oxford University Press is a department of the University of Oxford.
It furthers the University's objective of excellence in research,
scholarship, and education by publishing worldwide in

Oxford   New York

Auckland   Cape Town   Dar es Salaam   Hong Kong   Karachi
Kuala Lumpur   Madrid   Melbourne   Mexico City   Nairobi
New Delhi   Shanghai   Taipei   Toronto

With offices in

Argentina   Austria   Brazil   Chile   Czech Republic   France   Greece
Guatemala   Hungary   Italy   Japan   Poland   Portugal   Singapore
South Korea   Switzerland   Thailand   Turkey   Ukraine   Vietnam

Oxford is a registered trade mark of Oxford University Press
in the UK and in certain other countries

© Roger Lane 2006

The moral rights of the author have been asserted

Database right Oxford University Press (maker)

First published 2006

British Library Cataloguing in Publication Data

Data available

ISBN-13: 978-0-19-834975-4
ISBN-10: 0-19-834975-0

10 9 8 7 6 5 4 3 2 1

Printed in Great Britain by Basingstoke Press

Author's acknowledgements

Thanks again to Elizabeth Evans, for organizing sample answers; and to Hugh Lester
for 'keeping an eye' and tolerating inconvenience.

Acknowledgements
John Steinbeck: Extract from *Of Mice and Men* (Penguin, 2000), copyright © John
Steinbeck 1937, 2000, reprinted by permission of the publisher.
J B Priestley: Extract from *An Inspector Calls* (Heinemann Education, 1947), copyright
© Estate of J.B Priestley 1947, reprinted by permission of PFD (www.pfd.co.uk) on
behalf of the Estate of J.B Priestley.

Contents

To the teacher

Foundation Tier students are not that different from their Higher Tier counterparts, but perhaps they need just a bit more guidance and more of a push. This guide offers support for the ideas and activities in the *Foundation Students' Book*, repeating the strong, clear messages about the importance of structure, tracking and organization in their examination answers.

The pages of this *Teacher's Book* include:
- Mark schemes, to help students and teachers locate practice answers within a grade ban
- Sample answers, several of them showing some good exam technique but others exemplifying 'what not to do'!
- Grids, generally built around supporting bullet-points from exam questions, offering students an obvious structure to responses
- Tasks that focus on working with snippets of text to make students aware of the importance of the selection and highlighting of textual detail
- Poster-type pages that might, if used in strategic places (classrooms, corridors, toilets...) continually remind students of key messages.

Of course, not all this support is available in the exams themselves! The point of 'scaffolding' is to help along the way, not for the students to be dependent on it at the end of the course. Students can be confident that the WJEC English and English Literature exams will not be trying to trip them up, but will give them every chance to show what they can do. So, they need to be able to think for themselves, but able to operate within a sound framework that will advertise their expression and understanding to best effect.

Roger Lane

1 PROSE READING

Mark scheme

This generalized mark scheme uses phrases that are widely used in WJEC examination marking. Teachers and students can work out into which of these broad bands an answer fits and where within the band it might belong.

Grades

u/G
- Nothing attempted or struggles to engage with the question and/or the text.

F
- Understanding of the main events.
- Simple comments with occasional reference to the text.
- Unselective copying.
- Unsupported assertions.

E/D
- Simple comments based on surface features of the text.
- Awareness of more straightforward implicit meanings.
- Some reference to 'what happens'. Possibly some attempt to touch on the issue of 'how'.
- An understanding of the events and some sense of character and feelings.

C
- Appropriate material selected from the text to reach valid, sensible conclusions. Clear inferences based on textual evidence.
- Engagement with the issue of 'how', though possibly relying on some narrative or 'spotting' of key quotations.
- Some attempt to comment on narrative technique. Some grasp of writer's technique.
- Clear understanding of the events and a sense of a character's tone and attitude.

Unit 1.1   What are YOUR thoughts and feelings?

PERSONAL RESPONSE

Stone Cold by Robert Swindells

The question

(*Foundation Students' Book*, page 17)

- **What are your thoughts and feelings about Link's life on the streets?**
You must refer to the text to support the points you make.

This table can be used by students to structure a response.

Comment	Evidence from the extract
Link's life is very tiring – it's difficult to sleep	'If you've ever tried dropping off to sleep with cold feet, even in bed, you'll know it's impossible'
Link is always in physical pain	'...stomach cramps from hunger, headaches from the flu, toothache, fleas and lice.'
Link's life is also emotionally painful	'...homesickness, depression or despair.'
Link's life is lonely	
Link's life is uncomfortable	
It is boring – time passes slowly	
It is frightening	
It is hard to find food – Link is always hungry	
Link's life is unfair	
Link's life is unchanging	

Change the question!

(Foundation Students' Book, page 19)

- **What impressions of life on the streets do you have when you read this extract?**

Choose parts of the extract that you find particularly effective in creating these impressions and write about them, explaining why you find them effective.

SAMPLE ANSWER

(i) It is physically hard and mentally hard. It's physically hard because Link says it is very cold and difficult to sleep. It leaves you starving and makes you ill. It makes you mentally ill because it says Link is homesick and depressed.

It is a very lonely life. You have to deal with strangers approaching you all the time in the night. Link's life is lonely because he goes on about how much he's missing his mum and how much he wishes he was at home in bed again. You feel sorry for Link because he says he doesn't deserve any of this. He's just an ordinary boy and you know he's right. He doesn't really deserve to be homeless.

(i) "I haven't mentioned stomach cramps from hunger, headaches from the flu, toothache, fleas and lice". This list shows what you have to put up with if you decide to live on the streets.

Link says "What's that? Sounds like breathing. Heavy breathing, as in maniac. Lie still. Quiet. Maybe he won't see you." If you live on the streets you are scared all the time, wondering what will happen to you.

"A thought out of nowhere – my old room at home. My little bed. What I wouldn't give for – ." You spend all your time thinking of home comforts that you used to have.

COMMENT

The question requires a new focus – the streets, rather than Link, although they can't be entirely separated. In the first part of the answer, there is good focus for a while before comments switch primarily to feeling sorry for Link. Nevertheless, it is all relevant up to a point.

The second part of the answer is also interesting. The quotations are well selected and worthwhile comment is made on each one. There is some potential for choosing shorter quotations, linking them and developing comments beyond one sentence, but this is a sensible answer overall – probably borderline C/D.

Unit 1.2   How do characters behave...?

DEEPER MEANING

***Of Mice and Men* by John Steinbeck**

The question

(*Foundation Students' Book*, page 23)

- **How does the boss behave to George and Lennie in this extract?**

Consider:
- what the boss says and does
- how the boss says it and does it.

Tracking the text Important references to the boss have been underlined below. The table following the extract can be used to help structure a response.

> <u>The boss licked his pencil.</u> 'What's your name?'
> 'George Milton.'
> 'And what's yours?'
> George said, 'His name's Lennie Small.'
> <u>The names were entered in the book.</u> 'Let's see, this is the twentieth, noon the twentieth.' <u>He closed the book. 'Where you boys been working?'</u>
>   'Up around Weed,' said George.
>   'You too?' To Lennie.
>   'Yeah, him too,' said George.
>   <u>The boss pointed a playful finger at Lennie. 'He ain't much of a talker, is he?'</u>
>   'No, he ain't, but he's sure a hell of a good worker. Strong as a bull.'
>   Lennie smiled to himself. 'Strong as a bull,' he repeated.
>   George scowled at him, and Lennie dropped his head in shame at having forgotten.
>   <u>The boss said suddenly, 'Listen, Small!'</u> Lennie raised his head. <u>'What can you do?'</u>
>   In a panic, Lennie looked at George for help. 'He can do anything you tell him,' said George. 'He's a good skinner. He can rassel grain-bags, drive a cultivator. He can do anything. Just give him a try.'

The boss turned to George. 'Then why don't you let him answer? What you trying to put over?'

George broke in loudly, 'Oh! I ain't saying he's bright. He ain't. But I say he's a god-damn good worker. He can put up a four-hundred-pound bale.'

The boss deliberately put the little book in his pocket. He hooked his thumbs in his belt and squinted one eye nearly closed. 'Say – what you sellin'?'

'Huh?'

'I said what stake you got in this guy? You takin' his pay away from him?'

'No, 'course I ain't. Why ya think I'm sellin' him out?'

'Well, I never seen one guy take so much trouble for another guy. I just like to know what your interest is.'

George said, 'He's my . . . cousin. I told his old lady I'd take care of him. He got kicked in the head by a horse when he was a kid. He's awright. Just ain't bright. But he can do anything you tell him.'

The boss turned half away. 'Well, God knows he don't need any brains to buck barley bags. But don't you try to put nothing over, Milton. I got my eye on you. Why'd you quit in Weed?'

'Job was done,' said George promptly.

'What kinda job?'

'We . . . was diggin' a cesspool.'

'All right. But don't try to put nothing over, 'cause you can't get away with nothing. I seen wise guys before. Go on out with the grain teams after dinner. They're pickin' up barley at the threshing machine. Go out with Slim's team.'

'Slim?'

'Yeah. Big tall skinner. You'll see him at dinner.' He turned abruptly and went to the door, but before he went out he turned and looked for a long moment at the two men.

When the sound of his footsteps had died away, George turned on Lennie. 'So you wasn't gonna say a word. You was gonna leave your big flapper shut and leave me do the talkin'. Damn near lost us the job.'

Lennie stared hopelessly at his hands. 'I forgot, George.'

'Yeah, you forgot. You always forget, an' I got to talk you out of it.' He sat down heavily on the bunk. 'Now he's got his eye on us. Now we got to be careful and not make no slips. You keep your big flapper shut after this.'

What the boss says	How the boss says it	Your comment(s)
'He ain't much of a talker, is he?'	Playfully, joking, teasing	The boss is teasing Lennie and George
'Listen, Small! ... What can you do?'		He wants to hear what Lennie has to say for himself
'Then why don't you let him answer? What you trying to put over?'	Angry, suspicious	
'Well, I never seen one guy take so much trouble for another guy. I just like to know what your interest is.'		The boss is suspicious; he doesn't understand their relationship
'All right. But don't try to put nothing over, 'cause you can't get away with nothing. I seen wise guys before.'		The boss is warning the two men to be honest and not to try and con him

What the boss does	How the boss does it	Your comment(s)
The boss licked his pencil.	Purposefully	He means business
The boss pointed a playful finger at Lennie.	Playfully	
The boss deliberately put the little book in his pocket. He hooked his thumbs in his belt and squinted one eye nearly closed.		The boss is giving them his full attention because he is suspicious about them
The boss turned half away.		The boss is quite satisfied with George's answers, even though he is still a little suspicious
He turned abruptly and went to the door, but before he went out he turned and looked for a long moment at the two men.		He is a little angry and unsure about George and Lennie

Change the question!

(*Foundation Students' Book*, page 26)

- **How does George react when he is interviewed by the boss?**

Consider:
- what George says and does
- how George says it and does it.

The table below can be used to help structure a response.

What George says	How George says it	Your comment(s)
'His name's Lennie Small.'		
'Yeah, him too.'		
'Huh?'		
'No, 'course I ain't. Why ya think I'm sellin' him out?'		
'So you wasn't gonna say a word. You was gonna leave your big flapper shut and leave me do the talkin'. Damn near lost us the job.'		

What George does	How George does it	Your comment(s)
George said, 'His name's Lennie Small.'		
'Yeah, him too,' said George.		
George scowled at him...		
When the sound of his footsteps had died away, George turned on Lennie.		
He sat down heavily on the bunk.		

SAMPLE ANSWER

George really panics when he's talking to the boss. He speaks firmly mostly and answers all of the questions very quickly. George is desperate for the job and really doesn't want Lennie to say or do anything that might jeopardise them from getting the job there. George seems to be quite confident at the start of the interview. He answers all of the boss's questions quite easily. But George makes sure that Lennie doesn't say anything to the boss. ' "You too?" to Lennie. "Yeah, him too," said George.' George is really worried that Lennie will give the game away and stop them from getting the job.

George is determined to make him and Lennie look really good in the interview. He knows that Lennie isn't very clever but instead makes him sound like a really good worker, 'The boss pointed a playful finger at Lennie. "He ain't much of a talker is he?" "No, he ain't, but he's sure a hell of a good worker. Strong as a bull." '

George is very protective over Lennie and doesn't understand when the boss has a go at him, thinking that George is stealing money from Lennie. This is when George has to lie and say that they are related and that he is just looking after Lennie as a favour for his aunt. This means that George is very quick thinking.

Even though George is very concerned about Lennie, he also gets really annoyed with him too. Once the boss leaves and they've got the job he has a go at him. "Damn near lost us the job." This shows how angry George is and George warns Lennie not to do anything wrong again, "You keep your big flapper shut after this."

COMMENT

A fine answer, closely focused on the text. This must be a secure C grade. It is clearly written by someone who has wider understanding of the novel, but who also closely reads the text on the page!

Unit 1.3 Look closely at the evidence...

HOW DOES THE WRITER...?

***Paddy Clarke Ha Ha Ha* by Roddy Doyle**

The question

(*Foundation Students' Book*, page 29)

- **How does the writer create a sense of childhood in this extract?**

You must refer to the text to support the points you make.

Quoting the text The following points cover some (but not all) of the comments that can be made in attempting to answer this question. Completing and using the table will help in organizing a response.

Comment	Evidence from the extract
Paddy and Edward are playing a childish game	We were flinging water at each other.
Paddy has a childish reaction to the jellyfish	I screamed. ... I yelled again...
Paddy reacts childishly when Edward pushes the jellyfish at him	'I'm going to get you.'
Edward carries on playing and ignores Paddy'	
Paddy resorts to name calling when he's upset	
Paddy has a vivid childlike imagination	
Paddy runs home	
Paddy cries as he's running home	
He wants a hug from his mother	
He's mischievous and wants the mark on his side to look really bad	

Change the question!

(*Foundation Students' Book*, page 31)

> • **What are your thoughts and feelings towards Paddy now you have read the whole passage? How does the writer make you feel this?**

Consider:
- what happens in the passage
- the relationship between the characters
- the writer's use of language.

SAMPLE ANSWER

Paddy doesn't seem very nice in this passage. He is a bit of a baby and likes attention from everyone. When he is playing in the water with Edward, he over-reacts when the jellyfish comes towards him. "I screamed... I yelled again I couldn't help it." He gets really angry with Edward even though it wasn't really Edward's fault, it was an accident. He behaves really childishly towards Edward and Paddy is not very nice towards him. "I'm going to get you, I told Edward Stanwick." Paddy is also childish because he calls Edward names, ' "You're a big spa", I told him.'

Paddy also comes across as being a big baby when he goes home to see his mother. He seems to be making a fuss over nothing. I'm not even sure if he was stung by the jellyfish because no one else seems to be able to see the mark except him. "There? Ouch! No, look; the mark across." His mother seems to be teasing him a bit about it, ' "What should we do?" She asked me – "Will I go next door and phone for an ambulance?" ' But Paddy seems to be taking it all really seriously.

Paddy definitely comes across as an attention seeker. When his mother is busy feeding the baby, he makes his mark look worse than it really is, just to make sure he gets lots of attention from her. "I pressed my hand into my side to keep the mark there." This is not very nice and not very mature. But I don't think his mother is convinced by what he does because she just carries on feeding the baby.

COMMENT

This is a fairly unsympathetic view of Paddy, forgetting perhaps that he is only ten years old and that the writer Roddy Doyle has adopted the difficult task of thinking and 'speaking' as the young Paddy. Nevertheless, the answer contains all the correct signals – quotations plus comments, consistently developed views, tracking from start to end of the extract. Perhaps it's not a full-marks answer, but there is enough sensible quality for grade C.

Unit 1.4   Imagine you are…

EMPATHY

'The New Boy' *by Geddes Thomson*

The question

(*Foundation Students' Book*, page 36)

- **Imagine you are Tam**. Later the same day you meet up with your friend Alec. You tell him what has happened and what you think of the new boy. Write down what you say.

For the following important events from the extracts:
- explain in your own words what happened (the 'event')
- explain how you **(writing as 'Tam')** felt.

Event	How you ('Tam') felt
The fight and the money	
The football match	
The English lesson	
Seeing the new boy for the first time	

Change the question!

(*Foundation Students' Book*, page 38)

- **Imagine you are Colin.** You tell your mother about your first day at your new school. Write down what you say.

SAMPLE ANSWER

My first day started out really well. I got on well with the first years. They seemed to like being around me – maybe because of the way I look. I'm a big lad with a tanned face and dark hair and they seemed to like that. The first lesson went well, or so I thought. I joined in with the class discussion and even managed to chat up this really pretty girl with dark hair. Even the teacher seemed impressed with me. He said I gave a very good answer!

Things seemed to go wrong break time though. We played a game of football and I was doing really well but then this kid called Tom tripped me up. He said it was an accident and I believed him even though I was bleeding loads from my nose and from my knee. But no one else seemed to believe him when he said it was an accident. Things improved after that though and I played really well. Everyone said so.

For no reason, this kid started fighting me after school I gave as good as I got though. We ended up being friends in the end because I gave him his money back when he thought he'd lost it.

COMMENT

A job quite well done. It's a longer than usual extract to deal with, and it's not easy to judge what to put in and what to leave out, so the coverage is quite sound. The response takes us from the beginning to the end with the key steps covered. You could say also that the cool, calm nature of Colin is captured, but you might argue that the piece would be stronger with a little more evidence of his true inner feelings. C grade qualities, but not full marks perhaps.

A tip for a stronger empathy answer? Start at the end of the day, rather than at the beginning – then you'll go straight into Colin's state of mind at the sharp end of the story. You can still cover the key parts of the text, but your selection will be sharper. You don't have to replay every kick of the football match to show that you understand its importance in the story.

Prose Reading

(ENGLISH PAPER 1 SECTION A)

THE BRAINWASH BOX

- Do not miss out any questions.
- Answer them in the correct order.
- Give equal time to all ten-mark questions.
- Stick to the text <u>and</u> the right lines.
- Select key details and comment on them.
- Work out what the writer is trying to say.

EXAMPLES

What are **your** thoughts and feelings about ________?

What are ______**'s** thought and feelings about ________?

What happens in these lines? **How** does **the writer** make these lines tense and exciting?

Imagine you are ______. Look back…. Write down what you say.

Track the text methodically

2 DESCRIPTIVE AND IMAGINATIVE WRITING

Mark scheme for descriptive writing

Descriptive writing pieces should be assessed by making best-fit judgements across and within the broad grade bands, and also across the two broad assessment groupings. In 'best-fit' judgements, weaknesses in some areas are compensated by strengths in others. For practical purposes, students could be advised to consider *content and organization* first, then to confirm or refine judgements by considering *sentence structure, punctuation and spelling.*

Content and organization	Sentence structure, punctuation and spelling
G/F • Some relevant content, uneven coverage • Some features of organization or form • Paragraphs may be used to group ideas • Some appropriate detail at a general level • Limited range of vocabulary	**G/F** • Mostly simple or compound sentences • Conjunctions such as 'and' and 'so' • Punctuation attempted where appropriate • Simple spelling usually accurate • Uneven control of verb tense and agreement
E/D • Content attempts to interest the reader • Writing mostly organized appropriately • Paragraphs logically ordered and sequenced • Some attempt to focus on particular details • Some range and selection of vocabulary	**E/D** • Varied sentences, compound and complex used • Some subordination for clarity • Some control of range of punctuation • Simple polysyllabic spellings usually accurate • Generally secure control of tense and agreement
C • Relevant, coherent, engaging, sustained content • Writing organized in an appropriate form • Paragraphs used consciously for structure • Well organized, detailed content • Effective range of vocabulary	**C** • Range of structures, varied sentence length/focus • Effective simple, compound, complex sentences • Effective, accurate range of punctuation • Most spelling correct, including irregular words • Secure control of tense and agreement

Unit 2.1   Pictures in words

DESCRIPTIVE WRITING

(Writing to inform, explain, describe)

The question

(*Foundation Students' Book*, page 40)

- **Describe a scene at a train or bus station.**

Get focused. Follow the instructions below to make some effective 'descriptive' sentences.

1. Write two clear sentences describing an individual waiting for a train or bus.

....
....
....

2. Write two sentences about two people waiting together on a train or bus station.

....
....
....

3. Write a short piece of dialogue (speech) that might fit into the description. This could be either a quiet conversation between two people or it could be a more public exchange or, of course, just an announcement.

....
....
....

4. Write two sentences on the weather and/or the time of year and/or the time of day.

....
....
....

5. Write one or two sentences describing some fairly routine movement on the station.

....
....
....

Change the question!

(*Foundation Students' Book*, page 43)

- **Describe the scene in an examination hall.**

SAMPLE ANSWER 1

As the students walked slowly into the examination hall bearly talking through nerves. The heat of the exam room hit them in the face as they went through the doors, all taking their marked seats. They sat down looking around the room that they would spend the next 2 hours in. The walls were bear, no colour or anything distracting. The hot sun beeming through the high windows shining off the white exam papers; they sit waiting for the exam to begin. Nerves increasing with every minute, wishing the exam could start so they could get out quicker into the cool breeze of the summers day.

COMMENT 1

This answer is on task, and quite well focused, but the sentence control is very dodgy. The student does not use 'as' properly in the first sentence, and in several others s/he uses '-ing' participles (e.g. increasing) without full consideration of the verb (i.e. it should read 'nerves were increasing'). It is also a little short and…what about paragraphs? They are so easy to use and it's wasteful not to bother. Spot two spelling errors too. Overall, this is probably on the D/E boundary.

SAMPLE ANSWER 2

All of us sat there, looking ahead at the blank black board, no one said a word, and all you could hear was someone tapping their pencial on the desk. Looking around the room there was nothing but a spair desk and chair, pushed into a corner. The door opned, and slammed with an almighty crash. The room fell dead silent.
I looked to my left to see a boy nervous and twichy with a bead of sweat trickleing down the side of his face. I didnt have a chance to look at my other collegues. The teachers heels clonked on the polised wooden floor and as she walked the movemend of her could be heard. She started to carefully rip open the sealed envolope, and the person who was tapping their pencil suddnley stopped. The room was humid and the air felt dry as I breathed it in. everyone turned white as the teacher handed out the papers with a slap on the table.

COMMENT 2

This is a better effort and a better piece of writing, but the errors are too frequent. Sentences are generally controlled, but the first sentence is too long, and contains a comma splice (i.e. a comma that should be replaced by a full-stop). Otherwise, the sentences are nicely varied and controlled, although bizarrely one of them starts with a lower-case letter. No paragraphs again, too! And then there is the spelling! How many of the 10 or so spelling mistakes can you spot and correct? (Two apostrophes missing also.) The spelling alone is keeping this below C.

Descriptive Writing

THE BRAINWASH BOX

- Focus on the scene.

- Don't tell a story.

- Don't generalize.

- Don't overdose on adjectives and adverbs..

EXAMPLE

Describe the scene in a hairdressing salon.

You should write about a page in your answer book.
Remember that this is a test of your ability to write **descriptively**.

Use a picture in your head – bring a scene to life.

Mark scheme for imaginative writing

Imaginative writing pieces should be assessed by making best-fit judgements across and within the broad grade bands and also across the two broad assessment groupings. In 'best-fit' judgements, weaknesses in some areas are compensated by strengths in others. For practical purposes, students could be advised to consider *content* and *organization* first, then to confirm or refine judgements by considering *sentence structure, punctuation and spelling*.

Content and organization	Sentence structure, punctuation and spelling
G/F • Basic sense of plot and characterization • Simple chronological writing • Content of narratives may be undeveloped • Paragraphs group ideas into some order and space • Limited range of vocabulary	**G/F** • Mostly simple or compound sentences • Conjunctions such as 'and' or 'so' • Punctuation attempted where appropriate • Simple spellings usually accurate • Uneven control of verb tense and agreement
E/D • Some control of plot and characterization • Some conscious construction of narrative • Appropriate beginning and conclusion • Narrative developed to engage the reader • Paragraphs logically ordered and sequenced • Some range of vocabulary, creating some effect	**E/D** • Varied sentences, compound and complex used • Some subordination for clarity • Some control of range of punctuation • Simple polysyllabic spellings usually accurate • Generally secure control of tense and agreement
C • Writing controlled and coherent • Plot and characterization convincingly sustained • Narrative organized and sequenced purposefully • Engaging narrative with shape, pace and detail • Detailed content well organized • Varied paragraphs linked by connectives • Some use of devices to achieve particular effects • Effective and precise range of vocabulary	**C** • Range of structures, varied sentence length/focus • Effective simple, compound, complex sentences • Effective, accurate range of punctuation • Most spelling correct, including irregular words • Secure control of tense and agreement

Unit 2.2   Telling a tale

IMAGINATIVE WRITING

(Writing to explore, imagine, entertain)

Planning a narrative This simple planning sheet can be used to help organize the sequence of events in a piece of imaginative writing. Either write down key sentences or make notes to prepare the plot step by step.

Remember:
1. Don't use too many characters – three or four are enough.
2. Control the time-frame – don't attempt too much.

Opening

Development

Ending

Change the question!

(*Foundation Students' Book*, page 49)

The following are students' opening and closing paragraphs for the alternative questions.

- **a) Write a story in which someone stands up for his or her beliefs.**

SAMPLE ANSWER

We all knew we were all different that maybe why we came to form such a close bond as friends. 'The crew' as we all knew it Tom, Chris, Bethan and I we were all so different. Tom was posh and well spoken, Chris was sporty and liked heavy music, Bethan was a full devoted Christian and I was a punk who found Bethans beliefs inspiring.

Bethan always argued about Evolution and how we were really created. I took all her knowledge in to one day hopefully be able to say in confidence Im a real Christian and Im not ashamed. I was finding this difficult with so many expectations...

...Bethan and I were closer than ever before like a tag team, I was a Christian but I never gave it my full I went to christian meetings and church but I never announced it publicaly I was ashamed. Bethan was getting picked on because of her love for god I didn't get involed until one day it hit me I'd much rather have a true friend like Bethan than friends who didn't appreciate my beliefs. That day I told those people what I believed in they laughed but at least im the one with faith and hope in mine I stood up for my beliefs and I've never felt better.

COMMENT

Sadly, there are only two things to say. The tale is a good one – realistic, interesting, serious and full of tension. The English is poor – it needs a careful re-reading, with detailed attention to spelling, grammar, punctuation and sentence structure. The frequency of errors in this writing leaves it in the D/E area. Many candidates will write less interestingly, but get higher marks because they pay attention to technical accuracy. Try a determined proof-read of it...and see what can be achieved in five minutes!

• b) Write a story about an incident that taught you the value of money.

SAMPLE ANSWER

Last summer, me and my parents went to visit relatives in England. We had planning on staying there for a week but by Wednesday we had all ready done everything. Whilst having breakfast on Thursday morning we were all trying to think of things to do. The clogs in my brain were spinning around when I was munching into my crispy, slightly over cooked toast with the nicest raspberry jam ever made. I remembered passing a rather large and bright, casino like games arcade. I asked if we could go there. Fortunately, everyone agreed so we put our shoes on and walked down the street until we found our destination. I asked my mother for a pound so I could have a go at the blackjack. I won a few games, then lost a few but then won a few more. About quarter of an hour later I found myself in a very comfortable position of being four pounds up. I was enjoying myself so much that I continued to gamble away. Another hour or so had passed and I couldn't stop winning. Feeling proud of my eight pound earnings I decided to move on to the roulette table...

...The ball was still deciding on what number to stop on. The wheel was now at a complete halt. The smartly dressed man called out 'black seven'. My heart sunk as I took a deep gulp. I had lost everything.
For the rest of the night I had to sit on the side listening to my aunty and mother babbling on about what had happened in this evenings episode of Eastenders while everyone else was out there having fun and enjoying themselves on the one armed bandit machines. That was the last time I ever gambled.

COMMENT

There are some errors in this piece (the odd word omitted or misused), but not many. There is a run-up to the main story that might not be strictly necessary, but it is done brightly and the main action is reached quite soon. There is a little bit of imaginative detail to set the scene, firstly over breakfast, then at the casino, and the sentences are consistently well constructed and punctuated (although it is very light on commas in more complex sentences). Overall, it is a sound piece, clearly expressed, comfortably narrated... and it deserves a C grade.

- **c) Running Scared**

SAMPLE ANSWER

He was running as fast as his legs would go. Scared what would happen if the dogs caught up. He now realized that climbing over the fence to get his frizbe back was a bad idea. But what sort of old bat lets her dogs chase you across the whole estate without calling them back. Thoughts kept running through his mind. Would the dogs stop chasing him soon? Where could he go? What would happen if they caught up?

All he knew was that he had to out run the dogs for just a little bit longer. Once he got to his den he would be safe...

...He could climb the tree and be safe until the dogs lost interest in him and wondered off.

His legs started to stiff up as he struggled to climb the hill, he could hear the barking of the dogs coming closer and closer. But once he got to the top of the hill he could see his den. A large tree in the middle of the fields. As he saw the tree he got a new surge of strength and carried on running. Once he got to the tree climbed as fast as he could until he got to his treehouse. The dogs barking below at the foot of the tree, then it hit him.

What if the dogs didn't go away. No one knew he was up there. How long would he have to wait to be rescued.

COMMENT

Definitely a game of two halves! Very little is wrong with the opening (just a couple of slips?), but the shape, control and accuracy is lost in the ending. Inconsistent – unlikely to get C.

- **d) Write a story which ends with the following: '...It was all I could do to keep a straight face.'**

SAMPLE ANSWER

Me and my friend were in really bad trouble in school because we had been playing football in the wrong place and we had kicked the ball through the window and smashed it. Only a couple of people had seen us but unfortunatly they went strait to the headmaster and told him exactualy what happened...

...The headmaster called us into the office and we both had to tell him exactualy what had happened but we both denied being near it. The headmaster called in the people that saw it and they said it was definetly us but as always we denied doing it. The headmaster asked us a lot of questions about it and we said no it was nothing to do with us but in the end he just came really close to me and looked me in the eye and the it was all I could do to keep a strait face.

COMMENT

The truth is that this is written in spoken English, and you have to be very skilful to do that effectively. This is just a bright little anecdote that isn't properly drawn out to be a showcase for the student's writing, which is what examination pieces need to be. Punctuation is restricted to full stops only (correctly used, it has to be said), while sentences are largely 'compounds', i.e. lengthened by 'and' and 'but', until the last one just keeps on going! Looks like an E.

- **e) Continue the following: 'He never thought he would make the front page of the newspapers…'**

SAMPLE ANSWER

He never thought he would make the frount page of the newspapers. He wasn't the type of person to. He came from a small house on kings road. His mother was known for being 'weird' as my mother would say, and his father well nobody knew about him. I think he ran of when Josh was little. Josh was picked on a lot in school, constantly. I never really understood why though. Okay he had a few spot and wore glasses, but it didnt mean people had to bully him. I felt sorry for him...

...Once I was at school and he wandered through the tall ion gates. He didnt say a word to anyone, but everyone talked to him.

'...Where you get that cut from Josh? Your mother been hitting you again?'

'...Hiya pizza face hows it going?' Every day he came to school and had the same abuse thrown at him. Even though I felt sympathetic towards him I never did anything to help him or tryed to stop anyone from doing things to him.

I remember the day the newspapers storys came out. Different headings and different writeups in each of them...

COMMENT

A good, serious story, full of meaning. It strikes an interest in the reader, with the background and dialogue well handled. Rather a flat last sentence, but the prompt/title is well handled in terms of the structure of the story. Too many avoidable errors, otherwise it would be a C.

Imaginative Writing

THE BRAINWASH BOX

- Think hard at the start.
- Don't write too much.
- Control the ending.

EXAMPLE

Choose ONE of the following titles for your writing.

a) 'And I hope you feel proud of yourself.'

Write a story that ends with these words.

b) Write about an occasion when you had to look after small children.

c) Jealousy.

Write about an incident, real or imaginary, based on the feeling of jealousy.

d) Continue the following: 'It was my first day at work and I had no idea what to expect…'

e) Living in the past.

The quality of your writing is more important than its length. As a guide, think about writing between one and two pages in your answer book.

Think your writing through to the end before you start.

Unit 2.3   The weakest link?

TECHNICAL ACCURACY

Sentences and punctuation

Sentence...or not?
Task 1 (*Foundation Students' Book*, page 50)
(Copy each item and write down alongside whether it is a sentence or a minor sentence.)

Answers
1. A crowded waiting room.   (minor sentence)
2   Children climbing over the chairs.   (minor sentence)
3. The clock strikes nine.   (sentence)
4. The door opens.   (sentence)
5. No seats available.   (minor sentence)

Simple sentences
Task 2 (*Foundation Students' Book*, page 51)
(Each of the following items contains two or three simple sentences that must be separated by full stops. Write them out correctly.)

Answers
1. I waited calmly. As usual my brother was late. Fortunately it was a nice, sunny day.
2. The day drags on in school. Everyone waits for the bell to ring. There is no laughter here.
3. Finally the bell rings. With a sigh of relief, we go home.

Compound sentences
Task 3 (*Foundation Students' Book*, page 52)
(Make the following pairs of simple sentences into compound sentences.)

Answers
1. The weatherman forecast sunny periods <u>but</u> it rained.
2   I could do my homework <u>or</u> I could go out with my friends.
3. We have a new teacher <u>and</u> he teaches English.
4. I was looking forward to seeing Eric <u>but</u> he was out.
5. Rachel passed all of her exams <u>so</u> she went out to celebrate.

Complex sentences
Task 4 (*Foundation Students' Book*, page 52)
(Fill each gap with one of the conjunctions listed above.)

Answers
1. Leah has been afraid of the dark <u>since</u> she watched that horror film.

2. <u>Until</u> Danny learned to swim, he would not be allowed in the deep end.
3. Dawn made the coffee <u>while</u> I answered the phone.
4. Tony nudged his sister <u>when</u> their mother turned her back.
5. <u>Although</u> Sian was tired, she didn't give up and she eventually won the competition.
6. <u>If</u> global warming is significant, there will be more incidents of extreme weather conditions in Britain.
7. You cannot say <u>that</u> I didn't warn you.
8. You will electrocute yourself <u>unless</u> you connect those wires correctly.
9. Ian had to complete his homework <u>before</u> he could go out.
10. <u>As</u> he was injured, Freddie had to return home.

Full stops and capital letters

Task 5 (*Foundation Students' Book*, page 53)
(Sort out the punctuation in each of the items below. Be prepared to insert full stops and to replace commas. Shorten sentences and replace words if you wish.)

Answers
1. The stairs inside the stadium were crowded with people rushing to get to their seats. It was the match that everyone had been talking about.
2. When I got to my block I walked up the stairs, and saw a sea of red shirts all around me. I could feel the excitement building up to the kick-off.
3. The whole crowd then erupted. He had scored and Wales were winning. The cheers rang louder than I have ever heard. The whole place was jumping with excitement.
4. All that Wales had to do now was play it safe. The whistle blew for half-time. We had scored at just the right time.
5. The guitars were still feeding back and making a shocking noise. I wanted to get closer to the stage. Suddenly there was a big crash from one of the cymbals, and they started playing another song. Most people started jumping up and down at the same time, but there were a few people who couldn't jump. They were just wedged in the crowd to fill a gap.

Commas

Task 6 (*Foundation Students' Book*, page 55)
(The full stops are accurately positioned in the following items, but some commas would add control to the writing. Add commas where necessary.)

Answers
1. He could resist everything but temptation, and this was very tempting. However, he had to think of an excuse.
2. Just at that moment, I heard the car pull up outside and I knew I was in deep, deep trouble. My parents, who were returning from holiday, would not be happy to see the empty cans of lager, the crisp packets and the broken pots.

3. Duncan was only little, but he noticed more than they thought. As the men moved the furniture, he saw one of them slip a necklace into his pocket. Next, the same man took a quick glance at a pair of Duncan's mother's earrings.

Question marks

Task 7 (*Foundation Students' Book*, page 55)
(Copy out these items, replacing full stops with question marks, if necessary.)

Answers

1. What did he see in her? If he wasn't careful, she would have all his money. Would he come to his senses?
2. The question was worth asking. Where had he been at the time of the robbery? There was a doubt.
3. Wherever he went, the dog followed. The dog had adopted him. Would he adopt the dog?

Exclamation marks

Task 8 (*Foundation Students' Book*, page 56)
(Copy out these items, replacing full stops with exclamation marks, if necessary.)

Answers

1. What a game! It was amazing!
2. Don't panic! In an emergency, keep calm.
3. He had never been to Africa before. He flew low over the desert. Unbelievable!

Speech marks

Task 9 (*Foundation Students' Book*, page 56)
(Copy out the following items and add speech marks as required.)

Answers

1. Queen Victoria said, "We are not amused."
2. "I wouldn't say I was the best manager in the business," said Brian Clough, "but I was in the top one."
3. The boss pointed a playful finger at Lennie. "He ain't much of a talker, is he?" "No, he ain't, but he's sure a hell of a good worker. Strong as a bull." Lennie smiled to himself. "Strong as a bull," he repeated.

Spelling

High-frequency words

Task 10 (*Foundation Students' Book*, page 57)
(Find three spelling errors in each of the following sentences. Copy out the sentences, correcting the errors and highlighting the key words.)

Answers

1. Rhys <u>does</u> not like school, but he <u>goes</u> every day, <u>because</u> he is the head teacher.

2. Sally took <u>an</u> apple for her teacher, but the teacher was not <u>sure</u> if it <u>was</u> safe to eat it.
3. Do not make <u>any</u> noise <u>until</u> the <u>first</u> bell rings.
4. She <u>can't</u> swim <u>or</u> run <u>with</u> her leg in plaster.
5. He <u>wants</u> to travel <u>across</u> the <u>world</u> in a rowing boat.
6. We lent them <u>our</u> tent, and <u>they</u> <u>kept</u> it for ages.
7. The plane took <u>off</u> <u>eight</u> hours late <u>from</u> Heathrow Airport.
8. He was <u>only</u> five years old <u>when</u> he <u>went</u> to Oxford University.
9. I <u>now</u> understand <u>how</u> to drive <u>a</u> car.
10. Becky <u>heard</u> that she <u>could</u> sing <u>and</u> dance on Broadway.

Homophones
Task 11 (*Foundation Students' Book*, page 58)
(Here are some common homophones. Copy out the sentences carefully, filling the gap each time with the correct word. For extra emphasis, underline or highlight the key words.)

Answers
1. The <u>two</u> sisters were <u>too</u> excited <u>to</u> eat their breakfast.
2. That cat of mine! <u>It's</u> lucky to be alive. <u>Its</u> head was stuck up a drainpipe.
3. We <u>know</u> what the problem is, but so far <u>no</u> answer has been found.
4. I <u>hear</u> that the Queen stayed <u>here</u> last week.
5. He was naturally left-handed, but he learned to <u>write</u> with his <u>right</u> hand.
6. We <u>knew</u> there would be trouble when the <u>new</u> boy arrived.
7. <u>Whose</u> book is this? <u>Who's</u> responsible for the damage?
8. He went to town <u>by</u> bus to <u>buy</u> all his Christmas presents.
9. He did not know <u>where</u> the trousers were that he wanted to <u>wear</u>.
10. As he <u>passed</u> the young people, he wondered where the <u>past</u> fifty years had gone.

Task 12 (*Foundation Students' Book*, page 58)
(The following groups of words are mostly not precise homophones but, in practice, the way they are often pronounced leads to confusion in writing. Copy these sentences, filling the gap each time with the correct word.)

Answers
1. <u>We're</u> all going on holiday to Tenerife. <u>Where</u> are you going? You said you <u>were</u> going to Tenby.
2. <u>They're</u> a disgrace. <u>Their</u> behaviour is awful. <u>There</u> can be no excuse.
3. I could<u>'ve</u> won a lot <u>of</u> money. I nearly fell <u>off</u> my chair at the thought.
4. <u>As</u> Lennie was so successful last year, he <u>has</u> been invited again this year. He <u>has</u> natural ability <u>as</u> a sword swallower.
5. '<u>You're</u> a handsome guy. <u>Your</u> looks will be <u>your</u> fortune,' Gary said, looking at himself in the mirror.
6. If you remain <u>quiet</u> for a few minutes, it is <u>quite</u> likely that I will let you go on time.
7. Is this really <u>his</u> work? <u>His</u> handwriting <u>is</u> different.
8. He is about to <u>lose</u> a tooth. It is becoming <u>loose</u>.

9. After driving for so long, he was undoubtedly <u>weary</u>. His passenger was <u>wary</u> of him losing concentration.
10. <u>Are</u> these <u>our</u> suitcases or do they belong to him?

Vowel choices
Task 13 (*Foundation Students' Book*, page 59)
(Each of the following has an incorrect use of vowels. Write the correct spellings.)

Answers

believe	speech	experience	repair	field
boring	receive	serious	enjoyed	involved
steady	favourite	guard	usually	pretty
building	guilty	describe	disease	colour

Double consonants
Task 14 (*Foundation Students' Book*, page 60)
(Double consonants are wrongly used, or missing, below. Write the correct spellings.)

Answers

tomorrow	disappointed	disappeared	professional
together	occasion	opposite	struggle annoying running

Irregular plurals
Task 15 (*Foundation Students' Book*, page 60)
(The plurals below show misunderstanding of spelling groups and patterns. Write the correct version of each word.)

Answers

countries   charities   families   trolleys   addresses
monkeys   boxes   centuries   thieves   toys

Word endings
Task 16 (*Foundation Students' Book*, page 61)
(Look out for familiar word endings and correct the following spellings.)

Answers

bothered   jumped   taking   handful   happened   grateful
driving   bullied   break   uncle   favourite   vehicle
sentence   regularly   beautiful   frightened   occasionally   finally
pleasant   unfortunately   opened   probably   lonely   happiness
anxious   audible   sincerely   shaky   previous   option

Silent letters
Task 17 (*Foundation Students' Book*, page 61)
(In this task you have to insert the missing silent letter and/or adjust other letters.)

Answers

subtle	sign	writing	wheel	ghost
debt	climbed	island	salmon	knife

Polysyllabic words
Task 18 (*Foundation Students' Book*, page 62)
(The following words are incorrectly spelt because of a misunderstanding of syllables.)

Answers

holidays	temporary	miserable	business	remembering
everything	performance	interesting	beginning	devastating

Grammar

Standard English and agreement
Task 19 (*Foundation Students' Book*, page 63)
(Rewrite the sentences below in Standard English.)

Answers
1. Mr Jenkins has been at the school for five years.
2. We dug the garden all day for ten pounds each.
3. We were trying hard, but we were beaten by half-time.
4. I always do my homework on the bus.
5. Jim lost his temper when he got the blame for something he had not done.
6. He and I have been friends for a long time.
7. They were the best trainers in the shop.
8. She and I have eaten all the food.
9. We did a lot of work in English this afternoon.
10. I haven't done anything wrong and I don't have any money on me.

3 NON-FICTION AND MEDIA READING

Mark scheme

This generalized mark scheme uses phrases that are widely used in WJEC examination marking. Teachers and students can work out into which of these broad bands an answer fits and where within the band it might belong.

Grades

u/G
- Nothing attempted or struggles to engage with the question and/or the text.

G/F
- Simple comments with occasional reference to the text.
- Unselective copying.
- Unsupported assertions.

E/D
- Simple comments based on surface features of the text.
- Awareness of more straightforward implicit meanings.
- Some focus on the question. Some awareness of 'how'.
- A simple preference (in comparison) based on appropriate textual detail.

C
- Appropriate material selected from the text to reach valid, sensible conclusions. Sensible inferences.
- Use of language beginning to be addressed. Some grasp of the writer's technique. Sense of shape and overview.
- Clear focus on persuasive technique. Effect on intended audience considered.
- Valid evaluation (in comparison) based on a range of appropriate textual detail.

Unit 3.1   Searching and finding

LOCATING DETAILS

The Story of a Hero

Change the question!

(*Foundation Students' Book*, page 68)

- **a) List five things the Nazis did to pressure Max Schmeling, according to the website obituary.**
  b) List five things that Max Schmeling did to oppose the Nazis.

ANSWER

Five things the Nazis did to pressure Max Schmeling:

1. Hitler had him drafted into the Paratroops.
2. Hitler sent him on suicide missions.
3. Hitler took Max to lunch.
4. Goebbels had lengthy conversations with Max.
5. On several occasions Hitler tried to persuade the respected boxer into joining the Nazi Party.

Five things Max Schmeling did to oppose the Nazis:

1. He saved the lives of two young Jewish brothers.
2. He refused to stop associating with German Jews.
3. He refused to fire his American Jewish manager, Joe Jacobs.
4. He opposed the racial policies of Hitler's Third Reich.
5. He showed extraordinary generosity and humanity.

Unit 3.2   Small picture, big picture

EXPLAINING AND SUMMARIZING

Hack Green Secret Nuclear Bunker

The question

(*Foundation Students' Book*, page 72)

- **What impressions do you get of the Hack Green Secret Nuclear Bunker from the leaflet?**

With the above question in mind, give your considered personal response to the following items from the leaflet.

The bunker today offers a warm welcome to anyone looking for a totally different day out.

....

....

Entering through the massive blast doors, you will be transported into the chilling world of the **Cold War.** Re-built in the 1980's at a cost of over **£32 million**, it was transformed into the blastproof headquarters you can explore today.

....

....

View original broadcasts to be transmitted on all TV channels prior to a nuclear attack.

....

....

Hear the sounds, even the smells of a working Civil Defence H.Q. at the height of the **Cold War**.

....

....

Before ending your eye-opening tour, visit the Bunker Bistro for your **survival rations**.

....

....

And don't miss our shop, take home a souvenir of your visit to the **secret** world of nuclear government.

....

....

Change the question!

(Foundation Students' Book, page 73)

- **What kinds of people is the Hack Green Secret Nuclear Bunker leaflet aimed at? What evidence can you find to support your views?**

Read the following and discuss thoughtfully the target groups who might be visitors to Hack Green.

*A unique and exciting day out for all the **family***

Kids *have fun too!...* **Younger children** *can have bundles of fun as secret agents, following the **Soviet Spy Mouse Trail.***

*Where **history** comes alive*

How to find the award winning bunker. North West **Tourist** Board

'...all this was going on only a few miles from our house!' (**Locals**)

Schools and groups *are welcome at special rates.*

Finally, what about **you**? Fancy a morbid, claustrophobic day out?!

Unit 3.3   Investigating the truth

ANALYSING PERSUASIVE TECHNIQUES

Incentives Unlimited

The text

(*Foundation Students' Book*, page 76)

Comment on the short extracts from the letter from Incentives Unlimited to J. Smith, a member of the public. Include from the items any words or phrases that you wish to comment upon.

CONGRATULATIONS.... J Smith!

....

....

If you've never won a big prize before, your efforts are finally being rewarded. Today you've been awarded one of four fabulous prizes shown below.

....

....

Our research indicates that you have entered a number of prize draws, competitions or sweepstakes but, so far, you have never won a worthwhile prize.

....

....

...<u>we have persuaded the Sponsor to allow us to give to you one of the items shown alongside FREE OF CHARGE...</u> provided only that....

....

....

Please note, Mr Smith, this is not a random prize draw or a competition. It is a <u>guaranteed</u> prize award ...

....

....

P.S. It is my duty to warn you that, if you do not respond by the deadline, I have strict instructions to re-allocate...

....

....

Change the question!

(*Foundation Students' Book*, page 79)

- **What image is created of Incentives Unlimited, the company that has sent this letter?**

Incentives Unlimited are trying to present a positive image, but perhaps they are creating a negative image. Are they supportive and can they be trusted OR are they cunning and untrustworthy?

Answer the question with the help of the planning page below.
Consider:

The content of the letter
(Explain what Incentives Unlimited are trying to do. What are they saying to J.Smith?)

The language used
(Select words and phrases and comment on them.)

The layout and pictures
(Comment on whether or not the layout and pictures help the image of Incentives Unlimited. Does the letter do the job for them?)

Unit 3.4   Black, white, and shades of grey

COMPARING NON-FICTION AND MEDIA TEXTS

Kip McGrath leaflet and BBC Education article

A table like the one below can be used to help organize information for compare and contrast questions. Students could use this one when tackling the alternative question.

	Kip McGrath	BBC Education
Purpose		
Audience		
Content and message		
Words and phrases		
Layout		
Headings		
Pictures		

Change the question!

(*Foundation Students' Book*, page 88)

- The leaflet and the Internet article are both about out-of-school study for pupils.
  Compare and contrast the two texts.

Consider in each text:
- purpose
- audience
- content and message
- particular words and phrases
- layout, headings and pictures.

SAMPLE ANSWER

These two texts are very different. The BBC one tries to encourage parents to help their children with their homework and school work. It starts by using comments that parents and children have probably said to each other. It also emphasises that fact that parents usually don't know what work their children have got to do, 'Poor old mum is doing her best, but doesn't quite realise the demands of the courses her daughter is taking.' This reassures parents that they are all going through the same thing and that the BBC understands this. The bullet points offer parents lots of simple steps to help them help their children. These steps are easy to read and offer suggestions for things that all parents can do, 'Ensure that your child does their homework'. This is a good article because it tells parents exactly what they should be doing to help their children.

The Kip McGrath leaflet is very different. It does not offer a lot of different ideas for helping your child. It just suggests sending your child to a Kip McGrath centre. It offers help with Maths and English and offers 'a free assessment to find out where the difficulties lie'. The leaflet says that everything is tailored to the individual child. Also the parents do not have to do anything, just drop their child off and pay for their tuition. But the leaflet is really clever and does not mention how much you have to pay, it just mentions all of the things that are free.

Both of these texts are for parents. They offer good advice and tips on how to help your child with their school work. I think the BBC one is better than the Kip McGrath one though, because it offers free tips for helping your children and there are lots of different tips that parents can do. The Kip McGrath one is just trying to make money and if parents want to help their children they have to pay.

COMMENT

Soundly organized. Comfortably avoids a muddle, although some opportunities are missed because the bullet-points are not used fully. The question this time does not require an opinion or judgement but requires objective analysis. Often too much is said about layout and pictures, but here, oddly, it is not mentioned that Kip McGrath illustrations suggest very strongly that you will have a good time being tutored. In contrast, the boy at home doing his work looks more than a little cheesed off! Clear C grade for the answer though, despite the omissions.

An exercise in sorting

Look at the extract below from the Kip McGrath leaflet.

- **Underline short phrases (no more than three or four words each time) in two categories:**
  (i) problems that children experience
  (ii) solutions that Kip McGrath Tutoring offers to parents

Use a different colour for each category. Try to find at least **five** phrases to write down in each column of the table on page 45.

> **KIP McGRATH EDUCATION CENTRES UK**
>
> Many children experience difficulty with mathematics at some point, either early on in Year 2 or as complex concepts are introduced in Years 7 or 8. Often, with professional assessment, the cause emerges as a misunderstanding of basic principles.
>
> In English, too, some children will struggle with reading and writing as a whole or with key elements such as spelling or grammar. As a first language or second, not everyone is born with an ability in the subject; and individual problems can be addressed.
>
> Many parents worry about how their children perform in these critical subjects, so at Kip McGrath our professional tutors are trained in exactly these areas. We'll find the cause of the trouble, and then create a workplan to address the main issues.
>
> We have over 25 years experience helping children rekindle motivation, renew self-esteem and find the way to better exam results. Children do not merely learn and succeed, they learn to succeed; a skill that often helps performance in other subjects.

Problems	Solutions

Non-fiction and Media Reading

(ENGLISH PAPER 2 SECTION A)

THE BRAINWASH BOX

- Read the text(s), not just the headlines and pictures.
- Look at the key words in questions.
- Take care with your explaining.
- Don't get in a muddle between the two texts.

EXAMPLES

Make a **list** of **ten** reasons given in the article for...

What are the **writer's attitudes** to...?

How does the writer of the article try to **persuade** you...?

Compare and **contrast**...

Keep your answers clear, logical and organized.

4 TRANSACTIONAL AND DISCURSIVE WRITING

Mark scheme

Transactional and discursive writing pieces should be assessed by making best-fit judgements across and within the broad grade bands, and also across the two broad assessment groupings. In 'best-fit' judgements, weaknesses in some areas are compensated by strengths in others. For practical purposes, students could be advised to consider *content and organization* first, then to confirm or refine judgements by considering *sentence structure, punctuation and spelling.*

Content and organization	Sentence structure, punctuation and spelling
G/F • Basic awareness of purpose and format • Some awareness of reader/audience • Some relevant content • Relevant comment; basic analysis • Simple sequencing; some coherence • Paragraphs may be used for some order • Limited attempt to adapt style • Limited range of vocabulary	**G/F** • Mostly simple or compound sentences • Conjunctions such as 'and' or 'so' • Punctuation attempted where appropriate • Simple spellings usually accurate • Uneven control of verb tense and agreement
E/D • Awareness of purpose and format • Awareness of reader/audience • Reasons support opinions/ideas • Sense of purpose in analysis/comments • Coherent sequencing of details/comments • Paragraphs logically ordered and sequenced • Clear attempt to adapt style • Some range and selection of vocabulary	**E/D** • Varied sentences, compound and complex used • Some subordination for clarity • Some control of range of punctuation • Simple polysyllabic spellings usually accurate • Generally secure control of tense and agreement
C • Clear understanding of purpose/format • Clear awareness of purpose/audience • Appropriate reasons support opinions/ideas • Clear sense of purpose in analysis • Analysis/comment shaped for viewpoint • Ideas shaped into coherent arguments • Paragraphs used consciously for structure • Style adapted to purpose/audience • Effective range of vocabulary	**C** • Range of structures, varied sentence length/focus • Effective simple, compound, complex sentences • Effective, accurate range of punctuation • Most spelling correct, including irregular words • Secure control of tense and agreement

Note The above mark scheme is a composite of the near-identical mark schemes for transactional writing and discursive writing.

Unit 4.1   Aiming straight

TRANSACTIONAL WRITING

(Writing to argue, persuade, advise)

Change the question!

(*Foundation Students' Book*, page 91)

Letter writing

Imagine you have relatives living abroad. You have not been in touch for some time but you would like to visit them as it would be a cheap holiday.
Write a letter which would persuade your relatives to agree to your visit. Remember to set the letter out appropriately.

SAMPLE ANSWER

XXXXXXXXXXX

XXXXXXXXX

XXXXXXX

March 2006

Dear Bill and Ben,

I am extremely glad that you replyed to my last letter because before that I was begining to worry about you because you never replyed.

I have done some research and I have decided that it would be really nice for us to come and visit you. We have raised enough money between us to afford the flight over to your country.

We would love to come over and visit you as we have not seen you in over ten years. In your last letter you sent us we found out that you have a five year old son called Joshua. We also have a child but a girl called Bethan who is 13 years old. We have baught some presents for him so im sure hed like us to give them to him when we come over. We wouldnt mind staying in a hotel but we dont have the money so it would be really nice to stay with you even if we have to sleep on the floor. We would pay for food and drinks for the week.

I am really look forward to seeing you and I hope to hear from you soon. All our love.

XXXXXXXXX

COMMENT	Casual and flippant.

RESCUE PLAN	Get the context right. Who are you writing to? Where do they live? Get the tone right – consistently polite and friendly? Develop a few sensible, rational ideas.

But remember – you only get one go in the exam!

Change the question!

(Foundation Students' Book, page 92)

Report writing

Your town or district has received a grant to improve local facilities. **Write a report to the local council suggesting how this money could be spent to benefit the community.**

SAMPLE ANSWER

xxxxxxxxxx

xxxxxxxx

xxxxx

24th March 2006

Councilleur Jones

B****** County Bourgh Concil

B******

Dear Councilleur Jones,

I have recieved the pleasant news that we have recieved the grant. I have come up with some suggestions to how that grant should be used in B******.

I am a very keen sportswoman myself and my concerns are that the less known sports are financially suffering. My sport is fencing we only get one training sessions a week because we are unable to fund for anymore.

Sabre is the sword I fence with this is probably the most unnoticed fencing sword there is some real talent within the club in B****** we just need your support to get these potenial Olympic fencers a fighting chance.

Another facilites that could be useful for the teenagers of B****** is a concert hall. This would make B******* more appealing, we would be able to host bands and musical shows instead of just community shows. We need to kick start B*******'s appeal this would bring more enthusiasm to B*******..

Thank you for reading my letter I would be delighted if these ideas do crop up over B******* because it will help our economy and give B******* a piece of the action, the lime light.

yours sincerely

COMMENT	Talk about looking after number one!

RESCUE PLAN	1. Format wrong – replace the letter with a report. 2. Proof-read for errors and edit/organize the ideas. 3. '…benefit the COMM – U – NI – TY'!! Geddit?

But remember – you only get one go in the exam!

Change the question!

(*Foundation Students' Book*, page 93)

Speech writing

A debate is being held in your class on vegetarianism. You have to make a speech either for or against.
Write what you would say.

SAMPLE ANSWER

I am against vegetarianism. I believe there is nothing wrong with eating meat. If people don't like meat then thats there problem and they shouldn't try to make people feel guilty in eating meat.

Eating meat is good for the body and I don't think it is cruel to kill the animals. They are not of intelligent life and in eating a certain amount of animals can help keep their numbers down. So protecting the environment.

....

....

....

....

When the animals are killed for their meat they are not harmed and it is a quick and painless death. So eating meat is not bad, it is good for you. It gives your body the right types of protein that it needs for a long and healthy life.

COMMENT

Simple, direct opening, but that's ok. But then... 'thats there problem'... what's all that about?!

RESCUE PLAN

1. First paragraph – rewrite underlined part.
2. Second paragraph – rewrite underlined part.
3. Write another paragraph (between second and third?)

But remember – you only get one go in the exam!

Change the question!

(*Foundation Students' Book*, page 94)

- Your local junior school has invited you to produce a leaflet about road safety, aimed at 10- and 11- year olds. It should be informative and persuasive. Think about ways of getting your message across clearly. You may want to show where illustrations would be included in your leaflet, but you should not spend time giving details of these. **Write your leaflet.**

SAMPLE ANSWER

Safety

We all need to understand basic road safety because it is so important in life. There is basic information we all need to understand and its located in this brochure.

Roads

We all know how dangerous roads can be. I expect that the road outside your school has got clear signs telling people to slow down but if you take the points on board that I am going to suggest the things should be okay.

- It may sound childish but you must never ever forget to STOP LOOK and LISTEN when crossing a road. They are dangerous places. If you forget this then you may get hurt by a passing car.
- We all love to have fun by going on our bikes and by going walking, but we should always remember to wear a helmet and to wear bright fluorescent clothing when we go on walks and bike rides. Drivers need to be able to see you.

COMMENT

Surprisingly, perhaps, this is halfway to being a decent piece… but only halfway! There's an idea of how to use headings and bullet-points, and even of addressing the juniors directly, but it's all so uncertain.

RESCUE PLAN

Jazz it up a bit for the kids, especially the opening and the headings! Use some exclamation marks!!!!!!!! (But not too many…)

And remember – you only get one go in the exam!

Transactional Writing

THE BRAINWASH BOX

- Argue a case.
- Win the argument.
- Be accurate.

EXAMPLES

Write a LETTER to …

Write a REPORT about …

Write a SPEECH for or against …

Write a LEAFLET on …

Purpose, audience, format – but plan your ideas too!

Unit 4.2   Going public

DISCURSIVE WRITING

(Writing to analyse, review, comment)

Change the question!

(*Foundation Students' Book*, page 96)

Article writing: purpose and audience

- A national newspaper is attempting to educate its older readers in the ways of the young. It needs up-to-date, lively articles on hobbies and interests – from fashion to football, from music to model-making, from computers to cars, from tv to tai-kwando.
  Write a lively article for the national newspaper on what is happening currently in your hobby or interest.

Here are three openings to responses.

SAMPLE ANSWER 1

Go-Karting

Go-Karting is a fast and a thrilling sport. Each person races in 3 heats and then a final. Each person will race against about 30 other popple. Each heat you do depending on where you finish determines where you start the final from. After the final the top five receive a trophy and the winner gets roughly £100. over the last few years there has been a lot of cheating so now the rules are more strict. Every one must be over a sertain weight.

Everyone is now very competitive so a lot of people spend a lot of money on becoming quicker than everyone....

COMMENT

Good choice, good opening sentence, but then… What are the questions we are all asking? …How fast can you go? How much does it cost?
Sense of purpose – quickly lost.
Sense of audience – not really evident.

SAMPLE ANSWER 2

Computers

The days of the typewriter are gone, and the days of the supercomputer are here. Computers have changed so much over the last 50 years it is unbelievable. Computers are now in peoples everyday life, in your home, car, office. Everybody now has an access to computers. 50 years ago only the rich and cleaver people had computers.

Another big thing with computers is the internet. This allows people to buy their shopping or other goods without leaving the room. You can send letters which arrive at a persons computer who is across the other side of the world immidiatly.

Computers have changed in use. They were just for typing out letters. But nowadays it is used for everything, not just letters. The latest graphics allows children to play games with such good details it is as though they are watching TV.

Computers are changing so much even now that if you buy a new computer with the latest technology, but by next month they will be out of date...

COMMENT

Choice is not a particularly good one – it's not easy writing about computers, because we have quickly taken them for granted. Consistent reporting tone, which works OK although it doesn't really engage the reader.
Sense of purpose – uncertain
Sense of audience – neutral

SAMPLE ANSWER 3

Fashion Crazed Nation

From poppers to panchos and skinny fit jeans. The nation we live in today is fashion crazy, new trends are fading in and out of fashion like the tides. Teenagers are always under a social catogery that gives them a type of outfit that is in to the catougoury. All children and teenagers must have the latest fashion accessories and the latest craze of clothes...

If you parents are worried about the cost of fashion there are some bargins out there and customizing clothing has been in fashion. It become harder for teenagers to become unique. We all like to have the clothes that make us look good without the extursionant prices.

COMMENT

From good to bad in no time at all. It's not so much the spelling, more the sentences. The opening non-sentence works OK, but by the third 'sentence' it's a struggle.
Sense of purpose – in and out (some hint of a topical review)
Sense of audience – quite good

- Now write lively opening paragraphs on the three topics above:
    Go-Karting
    Computers
    Fashion.

- Then choose your own topic for the same treatment.

- Finally, to prove a point, choose a very (apparently) boring hobby and make it seem the most exciting thing since sliced bread!

A note on review writing

The poster for this unit invites students to write a review. A review is usually an article in which the writer gives his or her considered opinion, with details to back it up.

Another type of review looks back on a topic over a fixed period of time, e.g. a review of the football season.

Discursive Writing

THE BRAINWASH BOX

- Be topical.

- Be enthusiastic.

- Be interesting.

- Be accurate.

- Avoid vague comments.

EXAMPLE

Write a review of a book, film or CD for a magazine that is read by people of your age.

Your review should include:
- details about the book, film or CD you have chosen
- comments on its strengths, if any
- comments on its weaknesses, if any
- a clear recommendation.

The quality of your writing is more important than its length. You should write one or two pages in your answer book.

Give your discursive writing a sense of purpose and audience – do it for real!

Unit 4.3 Shame about the English...

TECHNICAL ACCURACY

Sentences and punctuation

Task 1

(*Foundation Students' Book*, page 98
Punctuate the following with full stops only. Then add commas to the three paragraphs.)

Answers

(paragraph 1)
   Hi. I'm phoning up about the topic of smoking in public. I have very mixed feelings about this topic. Firstly, I'm a non-smoker myself. But it doesn't really bother me whether or not someone around me is smoking, apart from when I'm in restaurants. Then the smoke really gets to me. I hate it when you're going to sit down to have a meal, when the people on the table behind you start to smoke. It really puts you off. Surely they can wait until they've gone, or have the decency to get up and go and smoke outside.

(paragraph 2)
   Another thing I hate about smoking in public is when someone gets on the public transport and begins to smoke, when there are plenty of signs up to inform them that there is no smoking on the transport. But these ignorant people choose to ignore the signs and do exactly the opposite. Surely they could have had a cigarette before they got on the bus or wait a few minutes until they get off.

(paragraph 3)
   I don't mind people smoking. They know the health risks and are willing to take the risk, so if they want to go around killing themselves, let them, just have the decency not to go around killing other people by passive smoking.

Paragraphs

Task 2

(*Foundation Students' Book*, page 100
Decide where the paragraphs should start and finish in the following letter. There are **seven** paragraphs in the original letter, all properly indented. Copy out the opening (**topic**) sentences to the seven paragraphs.)

Answer

95 Brush Street
Howton
England

17/08/05

The Editor
Daily Star Newspaper
London
WC1 3EE

Dear Sir/Madam,

   I am writing to you in response to the letter you printed in Thursday's paper sent in by Mr Newebee! I feel this point of view is totally uncalled for and he does not deserve to have his letter printed.

   Pop stars, sports men and women, actors and actresses earn that kind of money because they actually do earn it. They are always working hard to perform the best they can and will pay the price for their fame. They will usually receive much unwanted press and criticism for what they do in and out of work. They usually have busy schedules and are especially working non-stop for very long periods of time. An example would be Jackie Chan who is fully booked right up to 2007 and he only earns half of what others earn. Don't you think he deserves reparation for his work?

   Movie stars and other famous positions that command high salaries do not just jump on the ride. They have to make themselves what they are and usually people actually pay to see them and become their fans. You see people actually make movie stars etc. what they are and if they like their work, people will see it/them and this will make their bosses money for which they will reward the star.

   Not all stars actually earn all that much. Some will rise and some will fall, but the majority in the business will hardly earn anything. This is down to the pessimistic view of the public. So stop complaining about the stars just grabbing money. They deserve what they get.

Stars work hard to get where they are and even harder to stay there. You don't complain when an athlete wins gold for England, but you complain about the money they get. You are very irate about the way you think and act, which can be very annoying. You also know that most stars will attend charity events and usually donate money to good causes. An example of this is Elton John, look what he does, probably more than you do and he earns a lot to, but he gives 25% to charity, so is he deserving of his fees?

In short, you must argue that the stars push their way to the top and through hardships to get where they are today and I commend them and think they deserve every single penny they get.

I ask that you (The Daily Star) print this letter to voice my views and opinions against the other letter. Thank-you for your time.

Yours sincerely,
(xxxxx xxxxxx)

Spelling and vocabulary

Task 3

(*Foundation Students' Book*, page 102
Find 20 spelling errors in this piece of writing.)

Answer (22 errors shown)

STOP SMOKING NOW!!

This leaflet is specifically designed to target teenage smokers and try to encourage them to stop. Contained in this <u>leaflet</u> is help and <u>advice</u> on how to stop smoking for good.

[An illustration of a <u>teenager</u> smoking with a red cross <u>through</u>]

Why start smoking? It's not big and certainly <u>doesn't</u> look good. Today more and more youngsters are starting to smoke each day and <u>usually</u> the main reasons why are:

"My friends all do it so why can't I?"
"It makes me look good."
"My <u>friends</u> will think I am <u>boring</u> if I don't join in."

These tend to be the main <u>reasons</u> why most <u>people</u> do start to smoke. Well <u>they're</u> all wrong! All smoking does for you is:
1. <u>Increase</u> the risk of lung cancer and heart <u>disease</u>.
2. Puts tobacco toxins such as nicotine and carbon monoxide into your body.
3. Take away your <u>sense</u> of taste, make your fingers go yellow and make your breath smell.

Also
Your general heath and fitness <u>levels</u> will drop.

All of these things can be sorted out over a number of years if you
STOP SMOKING NOW!

SO YOU WANT TO KNOW HOW!

1. Tell <u>someone</u> you are going to stop so they can help you <u>avoid</u>
    <u>temptation</u>.
2. Get rid of all of your cigarettes, matches and lighters. Also
    make a list of all of the good points <u>and</u> bad points of smoking
    to see for yourself how bad it is.
3. Take up a <u>hobby</u> to take <u>your</u> mind off things, like aerobics or
    knitting.
4. If you feel the urge to smoke try chewing gum or something
    else to take your mind <u>off</u> things.
5. Once you have started stick to it, think of all the good points at
    the end of it.

FOR MORE HELP AND ADVICE CALL:
WALES – 01222 641888   ENGLAND – 0171 4873000
[picture of a fit and healthy teenager]

Task 4

(*Foundation Students' Book*, page 103
Read the report on Energy Saving and make it more formal.)

Answer
Note: Amendments made below are suggestions only.

REPORT TO SCHOOL GOVERNORS ON ENERGY SAVING
BY STUDENT REPRESENTATIVE

SAVING RESOURCES
   Pupils of this school are rather worried about the effects the
school has on the local environment. This report highlights ways in
which we as a school can change the effects of wasting resources
in the classrooms, and around the buildings.

SAVING WATER:
   The school wastes litres of water each week from misuse. The
following points identify ways in which valuable resources could be
saved.
1. Make sure all taps are fully turned off after use.
2. Only use water when necessary and don't waste it.
These two simple steps alone could significantly reduce wastage.

SAVING HEAT:
Heat is lost daily from the school because simple actions, such as closing doors, are not carried out.
To reduce the loss, the following points could be applied:
1. Keep all interior and exterior doors closed.
2. Only use heaters when the temperature falls below a certain point.
3. Fit draft excluders to reduce the heat lost through doors.
4. Fit double glazing in all rooms.

Points 3 and 4 would cost the school money in the short-term, but this money would be recovered in a short period of time because of reduced heating bills.

SAVING ENERGY:
This is possibly the largest waste of resources. Ways to reduce this are:
1. Ensure lights are only used when required.
2. Switch all lights and electrical equipment off after use.
3. Fit energy-saving light bulbs.

LITTER:
The school campus is constantly covered in litter and this is increasing every day. To reduce this:
1. More litter bins could be introduced around the school grounds.
2. Pupils could be made to pick up rubbish on school grounds as a punishment for dropping litter. This would not only discourage pupils from repeating the offence, but it would also save resources such as paper and lighting currently used in punishing pupils by issuing 'lines' and detentions.

If some or all of these recommendations were carried out, there would be a significant improvement to the school environment.

Grammar

Task 5

(*Foundation Students' Book*, page 106
Proof-read the following article and improve the accuracy of the
spelling, punctuation and grammar.)

Answer
Note: Amendments are suggestions only.

A Problem for Teachers or Pupils?

Discipline – the meaning for discipline changes. For schools, this
could be just one or two pupils shouting from the back of the class,
demanding all of the teacher's attention and changing the subject
of the lesson. But I believe that it is not merely the fault of the
pupils.

From my experience, my English lessons used to be the worst.
I was put into the bottom set reserved for the less able pupils and
those who would only care about themselves and thought they
were better than everyone. I was an A* pupil but only getting
below C grades for English. This was mainly due to the lack of
teaching in my English class. The teacher didn't understand
teenagers or know how to control the class. He thought that, by
shouting and screaming, he would get his own way. He would keep
the whole class behind, even though it was only a select handful of
pupils disrupting the lesson. After a few lessons like this, I started
to forget what was being taught and concentrated on other things,
such as my game console or a book I was reading. I had lost all
respect for this teacher, because he was not like other teachers
who could walk into a class and be able to speak and joke with a
class.

I believe a teacher must respect a pupil as much as a pupil
must respect a teacher. The teacher must be able to react with
the pupils, connect on a level with them to teach them, but also
remember to make sure the pupils understand what is being said.
However, this isn't entirely the teacher's fault. The handful of pupils
who shout, throw things or behave immaturely can also be blamed.

There are other ways to control a class. If it is one pupil
disrupting, then ask them to go to another classroom. Alternatively,
they can be sent to the library or to a senior member of the school
for one-to-one lessons.

If there isn't anywhere else the pupil can go, it makes the
lesson much more difficult as it acts as a domino effect and, when
one pupil starts to disrupt, another follows. A system is needed
which helps both pupils and teachers cope with discipline in the
classroom. If the behaviour gets to an extreme, there may be some
way for another teacher to teach the class. This would ensure
that work gets done and the pupils who want to learn can have a
chance at catching up and not getting left behind again.

Teachers all around the UK have to put up with a very small minority of students that attend school just to disrupt classes. What can teachers do to help the students that want to learn and achieve success? This is the sort of behaviour some teachers put up with just because they try to discipline the small minority as required. But what can the government, and what can we, do to help stop the small minority spoiling it for students and for teachers? How many people would stay in their job if they were threatened?

5 ENGLISH LITERATURE

Mark scheme

English Literature exam responses should be assessed by making best-fit judgements across and within the broad grade bands. In 'best-fit' judgements, weaknesses in some areas are compensated by strengths in others. The criteria for Specification A exam answers are those in the left-hand column, while Specification B exam answers are, in addition, judged against the criteria in the right-hand column.

	1. **Knowledge and interpretation of text** 2. **Exploring language, structure and form** 3. **Conveying response**	**Making comparisons** (Specification B exam only)
G	• Narrative with some misreading. • No exploration expected. • Simple expression of opinion with little textual support.	• Simple, unfocused expression of preferences.
F	• Some understanding of main features, including characters and themes. Generalized reference to relevant aspects. • May make generalized comments about stylistic effects. • Response conveyed in appropriate ways. Simple opinion about text, character, situation. Empathy simply expressed.	• Straightforward connections between texts made. Selection of some obvious features of similarity and difference.
E	• Narration with varying degrees of clarity and economy. Selection of relevant material. • Recognition of, and simple commenting on, particular features of style. • Addresses task and uses text to support views.	• Beginning to develop simpler points of comparison.
D	• More detailed reference to text – quoting, 'echoing' or paraphrasing as necessary. Awareness of sub-text. Some discussion of characters/relationships. Still reliant on narrative mode. • Beginning to see how different aspects of style combine to create effects, e.g. changes in mood and atmosphere. • Opinions related to question and conveyed with some clarity.	• Comparison and some evaluation of (e.g.) subject, character and impact of text.
C	• Detailed reference to text. Some probing of sub-text. Extended discussion of characters/relationships. Awareness of some of the cultural and social contexts of texts. • Some understanding of how meanings and ideas are conveyed through language, structure and form. • Points aptly supported by reference to text. Clear and structured response. Able to sustain character's view/voice with some consistency.	• Connections and comparisons (e.g. of theme and style) explored.

Unit 5.1   Points and twists

RESPONDING TO EXTRACTS

An Inspector Calls by J. B. Priestley

The text

(*Foundation Students' Book*, pages 108–110)

Practise close attention to detail by focusing on Sheila. Make a comment (or two) on each of the emboldened items below.

SHEILA: **(stormily) Oh shut up, Eric.** I know, I know. It's the only time I've done anything like that, and I'll never, never do it again to anybody. I've noticed them giving me a sort of look sometimes at Milwards – I noticed it even this afternoon – and I suppose some of them remember. I feel now I can never go there again. Oh – why had this to happen?

*****

Well, Gerald?

*****

GERALD: Why should I have known her?

SHEILA: **Oh don't be stupid. We haven't much time.** You gave yourself away as soon as he mentioned her other name.

GERALD: All right. I knew her. Let's leave it at that.

SHEILA: **We can't leave it at that.**

GERALD: (*approaching her*) Now listen darling –

SHEILA: **No, that's no use. You not only knew her but you knew her very well. Otherwise, you wouldn't look so guilty about it.** When did you first get to know her?

He does not reply.

Was it after she left Milwards? When she changed her name, as he said, and began to lead a different

> sort of life? Were you seeing her last spring and summer, during that time when you hardly came near me and said you were so busy? Were you?
>
> *He does not reply but looks at her.*
>
> Yes, of course you were.
>
> *****
>
> SHEILA: *(laughs rather hysterically)* Why – you fool – he knows. Of course he knows. And I hate to think how much he knows that we don't know yet. You'll see. You'll see.
>
> She looks at him almost in triumph. He looks crushed

Change the question!

(*Foundation Students' Book*, page 112)

(i) What do you think of the Inspector here?
(ii) What do you think of the way Sheila and Gerald respond to him?

Focus on the emboldened text in the extract to write an answer the question (i).

> SHEILA: …Oh – why had this to happen?
>
> INSPECTOR: *(sternly)* **That's what I asked myself tonight when I was looking at that dead girl. And then I said to myself: 'Well, we'll try to understand why it had to happen.' And that's why I'm here, and why I'm not going until I know all that happened.** Eva Smith lost her job with Birling and company because the strike failed and they were determined not to have another one. At last she found another job – under what name I don't know – in a big shop, and had to leave there because you were annoyed with yourself and passed the annoyance on to her. Now she had to try something else. So first she changed her name to Daisy Renton –
>
> GERALD: *(startled)* What?

INSPECTOR: *(steadily)* **I said she changed her name to Daisy Renton.**

GERALD: *(pulling himself together)* D'you mind if I give myself a drink, Sheila?
SHEILA merely nods, still staring at him, and he goes across to the tantalus on the sideboard for a whisky.

INSPECTOR: **Where is your father, Miss Birling?**

*****

… The INSPECTOR *looks from* SHEILA *to* GERALD, *then goes out with* ERIC.

*****

GERALD: … We can keep it from him.

SHEILA: *(laughs rather hysterically)* Why – you fool – he knows. Of course he knows. And I hate to think how much he knows that we don't know yet. You'll see. You'll see.

She looks at him almost in triumph. He looks crushed. The door slowly opens and **the INSPECTOR *appears, looking steadily and searchingly at them.***

INSPECTOR: **Well?**

Now write a response to question (ii). Make sure that you deal with Gerald and Sheila as two separate individuals, but also as a couple.

Your answers to (i) and (ii) should be of approximately equal length.

ENGLISH LITERATURE
Responding to extracts

THE BRAINWASH BOX

- Stick to the extract.
- Answer the question.
- If it's a play, remember the drama.

EXAMPLE

Read the extract on the following page. Then answer the question below:

(i)   What are your thoughts and feelings about __________ here?

(ii)   Choose parts of this extract that you find effective in creating these thoughts and feelings and write about them, explaining why you find them effective.

The quality of your writing is more important than its length. You should write one or two pages in your answer book.

Focus on the extract by annotating it.

Unit 5.2   Shaping ideas

DISCURSIVE ESSAY QUESTIONS

The question

(*Foundation Students' Book*, page 114)

Of Mice and Men by John Steinbeck

- **What do you think of Curley?**

Use the grid below to plan and structure your response. Make notes and/or write comments on Curley.

His first appearance, in Chapter 2

His relationships with the other characters

The fight with Lennie

The end of the story

The way he speaks and behaves

Change the question!

(*Foundation Students' Book*, page 117)

- **Which character do you have most sympathy for? Write about your chosen character, explaining why you feel sympathy for him/her.**

Use the planning page below to make notes and/or write comments on your chosen character. (You can choose a character from any of the books you are studying.)

The choice of character and why you feel sympathy for him/her

The situation that the character is in at the start of the novel/play

What happens to the character by the end of the novel/play

How the character behaves towards others

How others behave towards the character

The poster

Discursive Essays

THE BRAINWASH BOX

- Answer directly.
- Use the supporting bullet-points.
- Organize in paragraphs.
- Use details from the text.

EXAMPLES

What do you learn about the relationship between _______ and _______ at different points in the novel/play?

Or

Write about one or two parts of the play/novel that you think an audience/reader would find particularly amusing, and explain why they would have that effect.

You have time to think before you start to write.

Unit 5.3   Getting inside a character

EMPATHY QUESTIONS

The question

(*Foundation Students' Book*, page 118)

Blood Brothers by Willy Russell

- **Imagine you are Mrs Lyons. At the end of the play you think back over what has happened. Write your thoughts and feelings. Remember how Mrs Lyons would speak when you write your answer.**

Use the grid below to make notes for your answer. Think about:

Your feelings about Mrs Johnstone

Your relationship with Edward

Your feelings about all that has happened

Change the question!

(*Foundation Students' Book*, page 121)

- **Imagine you are giving advice to someone who is going to take the part of <u>Juliet</u>. Tell her how she should present the character to an audience. If you wish, you may focus on specific parts of the play.**

Think about:
- The way you think <u>Juliet</u> should speak and behave with other characters;
- The way you think she should show her thoughts and feelings.

SAMPLE ANSWER

Romeo and Juliet

For the part of Juliet I would advise someone to play her very innocent and young. Juliet is only a young woman and she has never been in love before. I would advise the person playing her to focus on this.

In the Capulets party near the beginning of the play I would advise them to play Juliet excited. She has a conversation with her mother and her nurse before the party starts, and she should listen patiently, but be firm with her views. She wants to marry someone she is in love with and the actress should emphasise this. Juliet should become excited before the party starts, especially when the nurse says 'Seek happy nights for happy days'. Juliet should be really looking forward to the party.

During the party, Juliet should be having a really good time. This would change once she meets Romeo though. As soon as she sees him, she should look like she is in love with him and be really happy to be around him. However, this should change to shock and horror once the nurse reveals that he is a Montague, 'the only son of your great enemy'. Then Juliet should be really upset and frustrated, 'my only love sprung from my only hate'.

But again, this should change when Romeo and Juliet do the balcony scene. During the balcony scene, the actress should portray Juliet as being all in love with Romeo and ready to do anything for him. She should also be quite determined and have her mind made up that she wants to marry him. 'If thy bent of love be honourable, thy purpose marriage, send me word tomorrow by one'. She should be really firm here about the way she feels about Romeo. She wants to marry him.

The other scene that is really important is after Romeo and Juliet get married, but before she knows about Tybalt's death (Act 3, Scene 2). During this soliloquy, Juliet is waiting for Romeo to arrive so they can spend the night together, 'I have bought the mansion of a love, but not possess'd it'. In this scene, Juliet is very obviously deeply in love with Romeo. She talks about him all the time and says things like 'when he shall die, take him and cut him out in little stars'. She is madly in love with him. The actress should also play this part very excited. She is looking forward to seeing Romeo again and cannot wait for it to be night time, 'Come, gentle night, come, loving black-brow'd night'. The actress should just play this very happy and excited because at this point, Juliet does not know what has happened to Tybalt.

COMMENT

There is some very good understanding of the task and the play here. It's a very engaging answer with a good instinct for the drama, attempting and succeeding in bringing the story and the character to life. Impressive. Very secure at the top of the mark range.

ENGLISH LITERATURE
Empathy

THE BRAINWASH BOX

- Speak directly as the character.
- Think like the character.
- Get the character's feelings.
- Remember you are looking back from the end of the story.

EXAMPLE

Imagine you are ________. At the end of the play/novel you think back over what has happened.

You may wish to think about:
- What happened...
- Your relationship with...
- Your thoughts and feelings about...
- The end of the play/novel

Empathy responses need the direct voice of the character.

Unit 5.4   Into the Unknown

POETRY APPRECIATION

'Tramp' by William Marshall

(*Foundation Students' Book*, page 123)

Selecting details Find at least two words or phrases in each section of the poem and comment on the significance of each of your choices. Sections begin:

> 'He liked he said...'
> 'And he liked he said the...'
> 'And he liked he said...'
> 'But he said...'

Change the poem!

(*Foundation Students' Book*, page 127)

'Peregrine Falcon' by Gillian Clarke

- **Write about the poem and its effect on you.**

SAMPLE ANSWER

Gillian Clarke makes the falcon sound like a killing machine, 'she is arrow'. She makes the falcon sound like a very powerful creature by describing it as very fast 'two miles a minute'. The falcon also sounds really scary. Clarke uses words connected with death like 'boneyard' and 'killing ground'. These words make the falcon sound like a merciless creature. This is also done by adding 'she wasted nothing'. This makes her sound very merciless, like she does not care at all about the bird she has just killed. The speed of the falcon is very terrifying. She attacks really quickly, so quickly that the remains of the body of the pigeon are 'still warm'.

Gillian Clarke uses similes that are very hard to explain. 'The pigeon bursts like a city'. This is not a normal way to describe how a pigeon has been killed. This could mean that the pigeon's body is like the layout of a city – a big burst of feathers and blood and body in the middle, and then scattering out over a wide distance. A city looks like this, with most buildings centred in the middle with fewer and fewer towards the outskirts. This is a strange way to describe it though and it makes the reader stop and think about what Clarke is saying.

The poet is watching the falcon and seems to be a bit afraid of it. 'I touch the raw wire of vertigo feet from the edge.' This sounds like the poet is watching the falcon from the edge of a mountain or a cliff. She is frightened to stand too close to the edge probably in case she falls. The falcon is not frightened of anything compared to the poet. It just flies straight for the pigeon and kills it. 'While we turn our backs,' also suggests that she is frightened. She is too frightened to look at the pigeon being killed and eaten by the falcon.

All the way through the poem, the poet refers to the area where this happens as the falcon's home, 'her scullery', 'her table'. This suggests that the falcon lives here and uses the sky as like her kitchen where she prepares her meals. This is again a strange way of describing the falcon, because it makes her sound almost like a person.

COMMENT

A very determined exploration of the details of the poem. Some very good comments and no attempt to avoid the difficulties the poem presents. It ends on a little bit of uncertainty, but the whole answer is very clearly in grade C, at the top of the mark range.

ENGLISH LITERATURE
'Unseen Poetry'

THE BRAINWASH BOX

- Read the poem carefully, more than once.
- Annotate the poem quickly.
- Cover the bullet-point prompts.
- Cover the stages of the poem.
- Comment on key details.

THE INSTRUCTIONS

Write about the poem and its effect on you.

You may wish to include some or all of these points:
- the poem's content – what it is about
- the ideas the poet may have wanted us to think about
- the mood or atmosphere of the poem
- how it is written – words or phrases you find interesting, the way the poem is structured or organized, and so on
- your response to the poem.

Apply your usual reading skills to the poem – don't panic because it's a poem.

Unit 5.5   Balancing act

ANTHOLOGY COMPARISON TASKS

The question

(*Foundation Students' Book*, page 132)

- **Choose two stories you think open well. Look at about the first 30 lines of each. Show how each opening is interesting for the reader.**

Use the following grid to help you with the structure of your answer. In an exam, if you get supporting bullet-points for a comparison answer, use them. Organization is an important feature of a good comparison response.

In your answer write about:

What happens in the opening

(Make comments on one story opening, then the other. Then make a clear statement, if you can, comparing the two stories.)

What we learn about the characters

(Continue in the same way, making orderly, controlled comments on each story, then commenting on similarities and differences.)

The setting of the story

(Continue to build an organized answer in developed paragraphs.)

Anything else you find interesting

(End perhaps with something that attempts a summing-up of each story separately and then link the stories for the last time. Try to say something new, maybe a personal comment.)

Change the question!

(*Foundation Students' Book*, page 134)

- **Some of the poems in the Anthology deal with memories. Choose two poems by different poets. Examine the ways in which the poets write about memories.**

Use the following grid to make notes and/or write comments on the two poems that you have chosen.

In your answer write about:

What the poet is remembering

How each poet describes the memory

How you react to each poem

Words and phrases you find interesting

ENGLISH LITERATURE
Specification B
Anthology Comparison

THE BRAINWASH BOX

- Back up your own thoughts about the stories and poems.
- Cover the two selected texts equally.
- Don't complicate by frequently criss-crossing the texts.

EXAMPLE

Choose two poems/stories, selecting an interesting character from each. Explain why you find each character interesting.

In your answer you may wish to write about:
- what your chosen characters do and say
- the relationships that your chosen characters have with others
- words and phrases you find interesting
- similarities and differences between the two characters.

Divide your time equally between the two texts.

6 EXAM TECHNIQUES

Unit 6.1   Focus on ENGLISH PAPER 1

KNOW THE EXAM

> 1. Check the front page to see how many minutes you are advised to spend on each part of the paper.
>
> Section A?   Section B   Question B1?   Question B2?
>
> How many marks for Section A? How many for Section B?

Answers
- Section A: about **55** minutes
- Section B Question B1: about **25** minutes
- Section B Question B2: about **40** minutes
- Marks for Section A (Reading): **40**
- Marks for Section B (Writing): **40**

SECTION A: READING (FICTION)

KNOW THE EXAM

> 2. a) How long do you think your 10 mark answers should be?
>   b) How much time should you spend on a 10 mark answer?

Answers
a) 10 mark answers should probably **average at least half-a-page** each of average-sized handwriting. The important thing is that you must be able to write a similar amount for all 10 mark answers.
b) You should **spend about 10-12 minutes on a 10 mark answer**. Work it out like this – you might take up to 10 minutes to read the whole passage, which would leave maybe 45 minutes to answer the 4 or 5 questions, including any 5 mark questions.

> 3. Can you think of an idea that will help you to stick to the correct lines when answering a question?

Answer
The best idea to help you to stick to the right lines for each question is to **mark off the lines on your question paper**.

> 4. What is the best way of answering a question with the instruction 'List...'?

Answer
The best way to answer a 'List...' question is to **use bullet-points**.
Note: Do not use bullet-points for other types of question.

> 5. a) What words at the start of your sentences will help you give a personal response?
>   b) What different ways can you think of to 'refer to the text'?
>   c) How will the bullet-points in the question help you to organize your answer?

Answers

a) **Start some of your sentences with 'I think...' and 'I feel...'** to focus your answer correctly when the question asks for a personal response.

b) When you are reminded to 'Refer to the text...', you are expected to **use quotations from the text,** but you can also **reorganize the text in your own words** (or *echo* the words of the text).

c) It may be wise to **follow the bullet-points by writing a paragraph for each bullet-point**, not forgetting to keep the original question in mind.

> 6. When you successfully use your own words in an answer, what does it show the examiner?

Answer

Using your own words is likely to show **deeper understanding** than just lifting strings of words from the text.

> 7. Do you think it is easier to treat the two questions above as separate tasks or to link the relevant words and phrases with the points being made?

Answer

As the 'double' question is marked as a single total out of 10, it is best to make one answer by linking the relevant words and phrases with the points being made. In other words, **link the 'What?' with the 'How?'**.

> 8. Apart from saying what has happened in parts of the story, what do you need to do to write a good 'empathy' response?

Answer

A good empathy response shows a sense of the character's feelings and **imitates the voice and attitude of the character**.

SECTION B: DESCRIPTIVE AND IMAGINATIVE WRITING

KNOW THE EXAM

9. Judge each of the following statements in turn. Decide which ones are *true* and which are *false*:

    a) In descriptive writing, you should imagine a scene in your mind and focus on it. *True* or *false*?
    b) In descriptive writing, you should write a true story. *True* or *false*?
    c) It is a good idea to use names in a descriptive piece. *True* or *false*?
    d) You must have lots of adjectives and adverbs in your writing. *True* or *false*?
    e) Brief snatches of dialogue are a good thing in descriptive writing. *True* or *false*?
    f) You should definitely have all five senses in your writing. *True* or *false*?
    g) You can write a descriptive piece in the first-person (*I, we*), the second-person (*you*) or the third-person (*he, she, it, they*). *True* or *false*?
    h) If there are lots of people in the description (e.g. a crowd), it is better to generalize about them rather than pick out one or two as individuals. *True* or *false*?

Answers

a) *True.* Focus on a scene. You should be able to see it in your mind's eye.
b) *False.* On two counts. Do not write a story for 'descriptive writing'. Secondly, the scene does not have to be a real place.
c) *True.* Names of people, places and things help to bring the scene to life a little. Don't overdo it, though, by naming everything!
d) *False.* Adjectives and adverbs are known as describing words, but it is not a good idea to depend on them in every sentence! Write naturally.
e) *True.* Dialogue is another way of bringing the scene to life, if used sparingly.
f) *False.* That's crazy! Sight, sound, touch, taste, smell? Two or three maybe, provided the reader can't see the join! Don't make it obvious.
g) *True.* Different tasks may require a different positioning by the 'writer'. In some, you may be part of the scene, while elsewhere you may be an outsider. Try different approaches in revision, including addressing the reader directly, with the second-person 'you'.
h) *False.* You must try to describe the details of individuals within a crowd, as well as the crowd itself.

10. Again, judge each of the following statements in turn. Decide which ones are *true* and which are *false*:

   a) You should start your piece of imaginative writing immediately because there is no time to waste. *True* or *false*?
   b) The opening of your story is more important than the ending. *True* or *false*?
   c) You should include descriptive details in a piece of imaginative writing. *True* or *false*?
   d) The more you write the better your mark will be. *True* or *false*?
   e) You should restrict your story to three or four characters. *True* or *false*?
   f) For most candidates, realistic stories based on personal experience work better than fictitious stories. *True* or *false*?
   g) It's a good idea to change the order of the exam questions and do the imaginative writing first. *True* or *false*?
   h) Examiners are prejudiced against certain kinds of stories. *True* or *false*?

Answers

a) *False.* Even though it's an exam, you have time to think. In fact, you cannot afford not to think. Writing without thinking beforehand is disastrous!

b) *True.* If you think about it, you want the examiner to be impressed from the start. At the end, the trick is not to ruin the ending, nor to appear as if you haven't finished your writing.

c) *True.* Although you will have completed your 'official' descriptive writing, you need to mix some descriptive detail into your imaginative writing for best effect.

d) *False.* Control what you write and don't write much more than the recommended two sides. Why race away and make lots of mistakes!

e) *True.* A good idea. With a smaller number of characters, you have a better chance to control and develop a piece of interesting writing.

f) *True.* Remember that a realistic narrative doesn't have to be *true* – it can just *seem* to be real. Mystery, crime, fantasy, etc. work only for a few people, and then only if they create something of human interest!

g) *False.* Imaginative writing is 'open' writing, so it could go on for ever if you start the exam with it! In any case, it's better to glance at the titles at the start of the exam and allow a nice idea to dwell in the back of your brain for the last part of the exam.

h) *False.* Examiners do have to judge the content and organization of writing, as well as sentence structure, punctuation and spelling. But they are trained to judge the quality of language and thought, not the topic chosen.

Unit 6.2   Focus on ENGLISH PAPER 2

SECTION A: READING (NON-FICTION AND MEDIA)

KNOW THE EXAM

> 1. Which of the following types of text might appear in this section of Paper 2?
>
> advertisements   brochures   extracts from novels   poems
> playscripts   leaflets   essays about people or topical issues
> magazine articles   newspaper reports

Answer

Advertisements   brochures   essays about people or topical issues
magazine articles   leaflets   newspaper reports

> 2. What important advice would you give fellow candidates for a search-and-find question?

Answer

Write your answer as a vertical list with bullet-points; collect at least ten items for the list.

> 3. 'Kim has had a _________ attitude to studying this term.'
>
> Think of as many different words that could describe attitude in a school report like the one above. Try to find at least 10.

Answers

Attitudes: good, poor, positive, negative, determined, casual, sound, flippant, improving, frustrating... and so on.

> 4. Think of different ways in which teachers try to persuade students to treat their work seriously. Find at least five.
>
> 'A teacher can try to persuade a student to treat his or her work seriously by ___________ the student...'

Answers

Means of persuasion: threatening, praising, flattering, inspiring, bribing... and so on.

> 5. Which of the following are useless as they stand? Which of them are probably saying something relevant to an exam answer?
>
> a) The brochure has a big, black, bold headline.
>
> b) The pictures in the brochure break up the text and make it more persuasive.
>
> c) The picture of the overweight couple links with the headline.
>
> d) The last word in the headline has a double meaning.
>
> e) The columns are persuasive because they are in sections with sub-headings.

Answers
a) Useless
b) Useless
c) Relevant (overweight couple)
d) Relevant (double meaning, but go on…)
e) Useless

> 6. What is the likely main **purpose** of the following types of texts?
>
> a) Newspaper report: to i______ readers
> b) Advertisement: to p______ possible customers
> c) Humorous article: to e ______ readers
> d) Argumentative article: to try to c______ readers
> e) Review (travel, film, etc.): to a______ readers
> f) Brochure (e.g. theme park): to t______ possible customers

Answers
a) Newspaper report: to **inform**
b) Advertisement: to **persuade**
c) Humorous article: to **entertain**
d) Argumentative article: to **convince**
e) Review (travel, film, etc.): to **advise**
f) Brochure (e.g. theme park):   to **tempt**

7. Match each one of the **explanations** a) – e) to one of the **comparison questions** i) – v).

a) *This question invites thoughts and feelings gathered together from the two texts.*

b) *This question asks clearly for comparisons as well as contrasts.*

c) *This question asks you to 'weigh up' each of the texts and to make a preference.*

d) *This question asks for the selection of the best bits from each of the texts.*

e) *This question concentrates on the contrasts in the handling of the topic in each text.*

i) Which do you think is more convincing – the article or the advertisement – and why?

ii) The images of _________ presented in these two texts are very different. In what ways are they different?

iii) Which aspects of these texts do you find effective in influencing your views on _________?

iv) What impressions of _________ do you get from these two texts?

v) In what ways are these texts similar and in what ways are they different?

Answers
a) iv What impressions....?
b) v ...similar and different?
c) i ...more convincing – and why?
d) iii Which aspects...effective...?
e) ii ...what ways are they different?

SECTION B: TRANSACTIONAL AND DISCURSIVE WRITING

KNOW THE EXAM

8. Consider the task above and answer these questions:

   a) What is the target audience for this particular task?
   b) Give a definition and example of a suitable 'well known' person for this task.
   c) Give a definition and example of someone who would not be regarded as 'well known' for this task.
   d) What general advice would you give someone writing an article that was intended to be 'lively'?
   e) Should the article have a headline, columns and sub-headings?

Answers

a) Young adults – teenage audience
b) Someone reasonably famous, e.g. David Beckham
c) Someone local, e.g. 'My mum'
d) Good opening; clear, considered opinions; informal 'voice'
e) Headline, yes; columns, not necessary; sub-headings, not essential but might be helpful

9. Consider the task above and answer these questions:

   a) Does the task require a formal or an informal letter?
   b) Think of a suitable person, destination and circumstances for the focus of this task. Give an example of a sensible choice to receive the letter.
   c) Should you encourage your friend to go or should you put them off going?
   d) Should you use selfish as well as unselfish reasons in your letter?
   e) Does this letter require 'Yours faithfully' or 'Yours sincerely' at the end?

Answers

a) Informal – letter to a friend (your address only)
b) Grandparents retiring to France or friend doing voluntary service overseas would be two sensible choices of context. Unemployed friend looking for work in China might not be sensible.
c) If they are sensible generally, encourage them to go 'for the experience'. Putting them off would suggest jealousy.
d) As a friend, be unselfish, but you might want to go and visit them! Understandably, you might not want to lose your best friend.
e) Neither is required for an informal letter, but Yours sincerely is less formal than Yours faithfully.

SAMPLE TASK

> **The Governors, who are responsible for running your school or college, are interested in the views of pupils/students.**
>
> **They have asked you to write a report, pointing out what you see as the strengths and weaknesses of your school or college.**
>
> **You might consider some of the following headings for your report, but feel free to choose your own:**
> - **Facilities and Equipment**
> - **Buildings**
> - **Range of Subjects**
> - **Out-of-School Activities.**
>
> **Write your report for the Governors.**
>
> Guidelines
> a) Write down the heading and date for your report.
> b) Write down the recipients (the receivers) of the report.
> c) Write down the sender of the report.
> d) Write down the opening sentence of the introduction.
> e) Write down a sub-heading, different from the ones suggested in the task outline.
> f) Write down three bullet-pointed recommendations.

Sample answers

a) Report on Strengths and Weaknesses of Grange Hill School.
   Published January 2006.
b) To: the Chair of the Governing Body
c) From: Simon Stacey (Year 11 Representative)
d) <u>Introduction</u> This report was commissioned by the Governing Body at its meeting of November 13th 2005. They requested that...
e) <u>Additional sub-headings:</u>
   - The school timetable
   - Homework
   - School uniform
   - Bullying
f) <u>Recommendations:</u>
   - The curriculum should be widened to offer more non-academic subjects.
   - The Senior Students Common Room should be re-opened following the approval of the new code of conduct.
   - A free water dispenser should replace the fizzy drinks machine.

Unit 6.3 Focus on ENGLISH LITERATURE Specification A EXAM

KNOW THE EXAM

> 1. How long should you spend on:
>
>   Section A? Section B? Section C?

Answers
- Section A – about one hour
- Section B – about one hour
- Section C – 30 minutes

> 2. Look at the sample questions on page 153.
>
>   a) Do you think it would be OK to write one answer to cover the two parts of the extract question?
>
>   b) Do you think you should aim for half a side or a side of an exam booklet for your answer to an extract question?
>
>   c) What are the differences between question (b) and question (c) in this particular sample set of questions?
>
>   d) What length of answer do you think you should target for question (b) or (c)?

Answers
a) Writing (i) and (ii) as one answer is OK, providing you remember to cover both parts – i.e. include details from all parts of the extract AND comment on them.
b) Aim for an answer of one side of A4 for an extract question.
c) Question (b) is an essay question requiring a personal response, backed up by details from each of the areas suggested by the bullet-points; question (c) is an empathy task, requiring the 'voice' of the character.
d) Target three sides for an essay/empathy response. Make sure that you write at least two sides.

> 3. Why do you think comments are more important than quotations in answers to extract questions?

Answer
Comments are more important than quotations because the text is already printed on the page, while the comments are your own ideas and opinions.

4. Essay and empathy questions

    a) How can you successfully 'write in the voice of the character' in an empathy task?

    b) What is paraphrasing?

    c) What is an embedded quotation?

Answers

a) The best way to write an empathy response successfully is to imitate the character's speech habits or patterns. Be true also to the character's deep and complex feelings about different matters.
b) Paraphrasing is using your own words to express the meaning of something.
c) An embedded quotation is one that is short enough to be placed in a sentence in your essay without disturbing the flow of that sentence.

5.

Differences between prose and drama texts

a) Prose has **readers**. It also has **descriptions** and **paragraphs** and **chapters**.
   Think of 'technical' words that you can use when writing specifically about a drama text, e.g. *actor*. Make a list of at least six words.

Similarities between prose and drama texts

b) Now think of 'technical' words that you can use when writing about either prose or drama, e.g. *narrator*. Make a list of at least six words.

Answers

a) actor, director, stage, audience, stage directions, sound effects, act, scene... (all are words likely to be used in relation to a play, rather than a novel)
b) plot, dialogue, narrative, narrator, character, relationship, incident, crisis, conflict, mood, atmosphere... (all are words that could be used about a play OR a novel)

6. Decide if each of the following sentences would be worth a tick from an examiner. Judge each one as *yes* or *no*.

   a) The title of the poem is 'Hurricane', which tells us that the poem is going to be about a hurricane.

   b) The title indicates literally the subject of this poem.

   c) The poem leaves you with a sad feeling.

   d) On the last line the poet says '...............'.

   e) The poet uses lots of similes and metaphors.

   f) The weather in this poem is a pathetic fallacy.

Answers
a) *no*. States the obvious – repeats the title.
b) *yes*. Not all titles literally indicate the subject of the poem – worth saying (if true!)
c) *yes*. Perfectly reasonable personal response (if broadly true!)
d) *no*. Copying out the last line is pointless.
e) *no*. All poets use similes and metaphors. Something more particular (and meaningful!) is needed.
f) *no*. Steer clear of 'pathetic fallacy'! It means the weather's in tune with the character(s). Write about the weather and the character(s), but don't go up a dead-end!

Unit 6.4   Focus on ENGLISH LITERATURE Specification B EXAM

KNOW THE EXAM

> 1. How long are you expected to spend on:
>
>   Section A?   Section B?   Section C?
>
> 2. In each of sections A and B, how long are you expected to spend on:
>   the extract question?   the comparison question?
>
> 3. How many marks is each of the extract questions worth?
>
> 4. How many marks is each comparison question worth?
>
> 5. How many marks is the Drama essay section worth?

Answers

1.
- Section A – about 55 minutes
- Section B – about 55 minutes
- Section C – about 40 minutes

2.
- Extract questions – 20 minutes each
- Comparison questions – 35 minutes each

3. Each extract question is worth 10 marks.

4. Each comparison question is worth 20 marks.

5. The Drama essay is worth 20 marks.